THE SPIRIT OF CHRISTMAS

All-Time Favorite
Gifts from the Kitchen

Edited by Jane E. Gentry

©2003 by Oxmoor House, Inc.
Book Division of Southern Progress Corporation
P. O. Box 2463, Birmingham, Alabama 35201

Hardcover ISBN: 0-8487-2566-2
Softcover ISBN: 0-8487-2836-X
Printed in the United States of America
First Printing 2003

Editor-in-Chief: Nancy Fitzpatrick Wyatt
Executive Editor: Susan Carlisle Payne
Art Director: Cynthia Rose Cooper
Copy Chief: Catherine Ritter Scholl

THE SPIRIT of CHRISTMAS
All-Time Favorite Gifts from the Kitchen

Editor: Jane E. Gentry
Editorial Assistant: Diane Rose
Director, Test Kitchens: Elizabeth Tyler Luckett
Assistant Director, Test Kitchens: Julie Christopher
Recipe Editor: Gayle Hays Sadler
Test Kitchens Staff: Kristi Carter, Nicole Faber, Kathleen Royal Phillips,
Jan A. Smith, Elise Weis, Kelley Self Wilton
Senior Photographer: Jim Bathie
Photographer: Brit Huckabay
Senior Photo Stylist: Kay E. Clarke
Photo Stylist: Ashley Wyatt
Publishing Systems Administrator: Rick Tucker
Director of Production: Phillip Lee
Production Manager: Theresa L. Beste
Production Assistant: Faye Porter Bonner

Contributors
Designer: Nancy Johnson
Copy Editor: Dolores Hydock
Recipe Consultant: Leah Marlett
Indexer: Mary Ann Laurens
Photographer: Ralph Anderson
Photo Stylist: Connie Formby
Editorial Intern: Terri Laschober

Cover: Orange-Macadamia Nut Cookies, Fudgy Joy Cookies,
Two-Tone Cookies, pages 102 and 103
Page 1: Vanilla Bean Loaf Cake, page 142
Page 4: Cranberry Butter, page 95; Ginger Scones, page 33

To order additional publications, call 1-800-765-6400.

For more books to enrich your life, visit **oxmoorhouse.com**

Contents

Season's Greetings

*Christmas is a joyous time—especially when you
give homemade food gifts from the heart.
Whether you're a beginner or an experienced cook,
prepare beautiful gifts of good taste with ease using
the great recipes and ideas in this volume.*

- Over 100 beautiful photographs
- Over 250 giftable recipes to choose from
- A tracking chart and calendar on pages 182 and 183 to record notes, favorite recipes, and gift planning

- Tips and quick ideas for gift packaging
- Helpful charts for every cook (pages 184 to 188)
- Top-rated gift recipe choices below help you get started making delicious treats for family and friends

Top 5 Hostess Gifts

Graham Stars, page 123

Fresh Ginger Pound Cake with Glazed Cranberry Ambrosia, page 147

Spiced-Up Party Mix, page 10

Almond Cheesecake, page 152

Chocolate Cheese Ball, page 168

Top 5 Make-Ahead Gifts

Creamy Ham Casseroles, page 66

Southwestern Breakfast Casserole, page 73

Sour Cream Yeast Rolls, page 52

Citrus Marmalade, page 94

Mexican Mocha Spice Mix, page 27

Top 5 Kid Pleasers

Marshmallow Cereal Pizza, page 160

Cinnamon Breakfast Rolls, page 54

Ornaments You Can Eat, page 118

Chocolate-Caramel Brownies, page 170

Chocolate Chip "Sandwich" Squares, page 159

Top 5 Editor's Favorites

Onion and Rosemary Bread, page 45

Cranberry Butter, page 95

French Toast Soufflé, page 73

Shrimp-and-Chicken Casserole, page 64

Cracker Candy, page 164

Cilantro Dip, page 21;
Spiced-Up Party Mix, page 10;
Cheddar Wafers, page 12

Merry Munchies

Nothing brings family and friends together during the holiday season like great food and company. And what a wonderful way to start a celebration—by giving an edible gift from this impressive collection of appetizers.

Caramel Popcorn

Caramel Popcorn

Package this crispy treat in cellophane bags tied with raffia for a simple wrapping. Hide the bag in a gift-wrapped box for an element of surprise.

- 12 cups freshly popped popcorn
- 1 cup blanched slivered almonds
- 1 cup pecan halves
- 1 cup cashews
- ½ cup butter or margarine
- 1 cup firmly packed brown sugar
- ¼ cup honey
- 1 teaspoon vanilla extract

Preheat oven to 250 degrees. In a lightly greased 11 x 14-inch roasting pan, toss popcorn and nuts.

Melt butter in a heavy saucepan. Stir in sugar and honey. Bring to a boil; boil 5 minutes without stirring. Stir in vanilla. Pour syrup over popcorn mixture, stirring until coated.

Bake 1 hour, stirring every 15 minutes. Cool completely; break into pieces. Store in an airtight container.
Yield: about 4 quarts popcorn

Rosemary Popcorn with Pine Nuts

For this recipe, you make herb-flavored oil to pop kernels in. Use leftover herb-flavored oil in salad dressings, marinades, sauces, or as a condiment with French bread.

- 1 cup olive oil
- ½ cup unpopped popcorn kernels
- 12 rosemary sprigs (6 inches each), cut into 2-inch pieces
- 1½ teaspoons sea salt, divided
- ½ cup pine nuts, toasted
- 2 tablespoons coarsely chopped fresh rosemary

In a small saucepan, cook oil over low heat 3 minutes. Add popcorn kernels, rosemary, and 1 teaspoon sea salt. Remove mixture from heat; cover and let stand at room temperature 48 hours.

Drain kernels, reserving oil; discard rosemary.

Place 3 tablespoons flavored oil and popcorn kernels in a Dutch oven. Cook, covered, over high heat, shaking pan often for 4 minutes until popping begins to slow. Remove from heat; let stand 2 minutes or until popping stops.

Combine popcorn, remaining salt, pine nuts, and rosemary in a large bowl. Store in an airtight container.
Yield: about 14 cups popcorn

Basil, Garlic, and Parmesan Popcorn: Substitute basil for rosemary and ½ cup grated garlic-and-herb Parmesan cheese for pine nuts.

Pepper Almonds

Save the cans from the almonds to use as gift containers. Simply cover the cans with holiday wrapping paper and trim with a wide ribbon.

- 2 cans (6 ounces each) whole natural almonds
- 3 tablespoons butter or margarine
- 3 tablespoons white wine Worcestershire sauce
- 1 teaspoon salt
- 1 teaspoon chili powder
- ½ teaspoon garlic powder
- ⅛ teaspoon ground white pepper
- ⅛ teaspoon ground red pepper
- ⅛ teaspoon ground black pepper

Place almonds in a medium bowl. Melt butter in a small skillet or saucepan. Stir in Worcestershire sauce, salt, chili powder, garlic powder, and peppers. Cook 1 minute. Remove from heat, and pour over almonds; stir well. Let stand 30 minutes.

Preheat oven to 300 degrees. Arrange almonds in a single layer on an ungreased jellyroll pan or baking sheet.

Bake 35 minutes or until toasted, stirring often. Cool completely and store in an airtight container.
Yield: about 2 cups nuts

Spicy-Sweet Pecans

Make two batches of these pecans so you can keep one for yourself—you won't be able to resist their savory sweet sensation.

- 2 tablespoons brown sugar
- 2 tablespoons orange juice concentrate
- 1½ tablespoons butter or margarine
- ½ teaspoon salt
- ½ teaspoon chili powder
- ¼ teaspoon ground black pepper
- 1½ cups coarsely chopped pecans

Preheat oven to 350 degrees. In a skillet, cook brown sugar, orange juice concentrate, butter, salt, chili powder, and pepper over medium-high heat, stirring until brown sugar dissolves. Remove from heat, and stir in chopped pecans. Transfer to a lightly greased baking sheet.

Bake 8 minutes or until toasted. Cool and store in an airtight container.
Yield: about 1½ cups pecans

Hot Peanuts

Spiced-Up Party Mix
(pictured on page 6)

Several popular munchies team up in this ultimate party mix that makes enough for gifts for all your neighbors.

>   1 cup butter or margarine, melted
>   1 tablespoon Worcestershire sauce
>   1 teaspoon curry powder
>   ½ teaspoon garlic salt
>   ⅛ teaspoon hot sauce
>   6 cups corn chips
>   6 cups freshly popped popcorn
>   4 cups cheese crackers
>   3 cups mixed nuts
>   1½ cups walnut pieces

Preheat oven to 250 degrees. In a medium bowl, combine butter, Worcestershire sauce, curry powder, garlic salt, and hot sauce; stir until blended.

In a roasting pan, combine chips, popcorn, crackers, nuts, and walnuts; add butter mixture, stirring to coat.

Bake 1 hour, stirring every 15 minutes. Spread on paper towels to cool. Store in an airtight container.
Yield: about 4 quarts mix

Hot Peanuts

This recipe easily makes two gifts. Buy two 2-cup tin containers of different colors and switch the tops to display a combination of Christmas shades.

>   1 to 2 tablespoons dried crushed red pepper
>   3 tablespoons olive oil
>   4 cloves garlic, pressed
>   1 can (12 ounces) salted peanuts
>   1 can (12 ounces) Spanish peanuts
>   1 teaspoon salt
>   ½ teaspoon chili powder

In a large skillet, cook crushed red pepper in hot oil 1 minute. Stir in garlic and peanuts; cook over medium heat, stirring constantly, 5 minutes. Remove from heat; sprinkle with salt and chili powder. Drain on paper towels; cool completely. Store in an airtight container.
Yield: about 4 cups peanuts

The Freshest Nuts

Nuts can turn rancid (develop a stale "off" flavor) quickly because of their high fat content. To avoid the risk of ruining whatever food you're using nuts in, follow these simple guidelines.

• Buy the freshest nuts possible. Look for shelled nuts that are plump, crisp, and consistent in size and color.

• Store nuts in the shell in an airtight container in a cool place.

• Refrigerate shelled nuts up to 4 months or freeze up to 6 months. Never store shelled nuts at room temperature.

Healthful Granola

Your friends will enjoy guilt-free indulgence with this granola packed with healthy oats, nuts, and dried fruits.

>   2 cups uncooked regular oats
>   ¾ cup uncooked hot oat bran cereal
>   ½ cup sliced almonds
>   1 teaspoon ground cinnamon
>   ¼ teaspoon salt
>   ½ cup honey
>   2 tablespoons vegetable oil
>   1 tablespoon water
>   ½ teaspoon vanilla extract
>   ¾ cup raisins
>   ½ cup pitted dates, chopped
>   ⅓ cup sweetened dried cranberries
>   ¼ cup sunflower kernels

Preheat oven to 350 degrees. In a medium bowl, combine oats, cereal, almonds, cinnamon, and salt. Stir together honey, oil, water, and vanilla in a small bowl until blended.

Combine honey mixture and oats mixture; stir until blended. Spread into a lightly greased 10½ x 15½-inch jellyroll pan.

Bake, stirring often, 20 minutes or until dark brown; cool in pan on a wire rack.

Stir in raisins and remaining ingredients; store in an airtight container.
Yield: about 5 cups granola

Peanut Butter-Granola Gorp

Pack & Ship

For a quick, on-hand gift, store this crunchy trail mix in small resealable plastic bags.

- ¼ cup creamy peanut butter
- ¼ cup maple-flavored syrup
- 1 cup granola with raisins
- 32 tiny pretzel twists
- ½ cup golden raisins
- ½ cup sweetened dried cranberries

Preheat oven to 300 degrees. In a small microwave-safe bowl, combine peanut butter and syrup. Microwave on high power (100%) for 30 seconds or until hot; stir well. Place granola and pretzels in a large bowl; pour peanut butter mixture over granola mixture, stirring to coat. Spread mixture in a single layer on a lightly greased jellyroll pan.

Bake 25 minutes, stirring twice. Stir in raisins and cranberries; return pan to oven. Turn oven off; cool mixture in closed oven 30 minutes. Remove from oven; cool completely. Store in an airtight container. **Yield:** about 3½ cups gorp

Peanut Butter-Granola Gorp

Parmesan-Pecan Cheese Bites

Layer these cheesy treats between waxed paper to place in an airtight tin for a useful and unexpected surprise.

  1 cup all-purpose flour
  ⅔ cup freshly grated Parmesan cheese
  ¼ teaspoon ground red pepper
  ½ cup butter or margarine, cut up
  2 tablespoons milk
    Pecan halves

  In a food processor, combine flour, cheese, red pepper, and butter. Process until well blended.
  Shape dough into 2 (4-inch) logs. Wrap in plastic wrap, and place in an airtight container. Chill 8 hours.
  Preheat oven to 350 degrees. Cut dough into ¼-inch-thick slices, and place on a lightly greased baking sheet. Brush with milk. Top with pecan halves.
  Bake 12 to 15 minutes or until lightly browned. Transfer to wire racks to cool. Store in an airtight container.
Yield: about 2½ dozen cheese bites

Make-ahead options: If you need a headstart on holiday gift baking, this recipe offers two options. You can freeze the logs of dough up to 1 month before baking (thaw in refrigerator overnight) or freeze the baked rounds up to 1 month before giving them (thaw at room temperature 2 hours before wrapping).

Antique Tins

Antique tin containers make whimsical packages for food gifts. Found anywhere from thrift stores to your Grandma's attic, they add a sense of nostalgia to a thoughtful gift. They may be worn, dented, or beginning to show a little rust, but these timeless treasures show character and can still be used for gift giving!

  Always line your tin with some type of protective layer like plastic wrap or cellophane to keep moisture and food from making contact with the container. This will prevent rusting and prolong the life of your tin. Place a layer of tissue paper on top of the plastic to hide the protective coating.

  If you're giving a dip or another food suitable for a small platter, position the food on the platter and fit it inside the prepared tin. And simpler yet, if you're giving cookies or another dry product, place them in a resealable plastic bag before placing them in the tin container. Seal with the lid and your package is complete...you don't even need a bow!

Cheddar Wafers

(pictured on page 6)

Place these wafers in a resealable plastic bag, wrap in unique fabric napkins, and deliver in a basket along with fresh fruit and a bottle of wine—a great beginning for an impromptu wine and cheese party.

  2 cups butter or margarine, softened
  1 pound sharp Cheddar cheese, shredded
  4 cups all-purpose flour
  ½ teaspoon salt
  1 to 2 teaspoons ground red pepper
  ½ teaspoon paprika

  In a large bowl, combine butter and Cheddar cheese. Beat at medium speed of an electric mixer until blended; add all-purpose flour and remaining ingredients, beating until blended. Cover dough and chill 2 hours.
  Shape dough into 4 (8-inch) logs; cover and chill 8 hours.
  Preheat oven to 350 degrees. Cut dough into ¼-inch slices, and place on ungreased baking sheets.
  Bake 15 minutes. Remove to wire racks to cool. Store in an airtight container.
Yield: about 10 dozen wafers

Italian Cheese Straws

Italian herbs lend a distinct flavor to these cheese straws based on mozzarella. Wrap them in a cellophane bag and tie with a ribbon for quick and easy transport.

  2 cups (8 ounces) shredded mozzarella cheese, softened
  ½ cup butter, softened
  1½ cups all-purpose flour
  2 teaspoons dried Italian herb seasoning
  ½ teaspoon salt
  ¼ teaspoon ground white pepper

  Preheat oven to 375 degrees. In a medium bowl, combine cheese and butter, stirring until blended. Gradually add flour, seasoning, salt, and pepper, stirring until mixture is no longer crumbly and will shape into a ball.
  Use a cookie press fitted with a bar-shaped disk to shape into straws, following manufacturer's instructions. Or roll dough into a ¼-inch-thick rectangle on floured waxed paper. Cut into ½ x 2-inch strips with a knife or pastry wheel. Place on ungreased baking sheets.
  Bake 8 minutes or until lightly browned. Transfer to wire racks to cool. Store in an airtight container.
Yield: about 8 dozen cheese straws

"Pinecone" Cheese Ball

Blue Cheese Ball

The belle of this ball is the whole package of crumbled blue cheese that's mixed with black olives and cream cheese and then rolled in crunchy pecans. Wrap it in plastic wrap and present it in a basket with apples or pears to cut into slices and serve alongside.

- 1 package (8 ounces) cream cheese, softened
- 1 container (4 ounces) crumbled blue cheese
- ½ cup chopped ripe olives
- 1 teaspoon Worcestershire sauce
- 1 cup finely chopped pecans

In a bowl, combine cream cheese, blue cheese, olives, and Worcestershire sauce; stir until blended. Shape into a ball, using wet hands; roll in pecans. Cover and chill up to 4 days.
Yield: about 8 to 10 servings

"Pinecone" Cheese Ball

Give this clever cheese ball in a sturdy box that can be easily opened—you'll want to show it off immediately. Be sure to place it on a platter for easy removal.

- 1 container (8 ounces) garden vegetable cream cheese
- 1 container (8 ounces) roasted garlic cream cheese
- 1 cup (4 ounces) shredded sharp Cheddar cheese
- 3 green onions, chopped
- 2 cups pecan halves, toasted
  Fresh rosemary sprigs

In a medium bowl, combine cheeses and onion; stir together. Shape into an oval; chill 2 hours.
Arrange pecan halves over cheese oval in overlapping rows beginning at bottom and working upward to resemble a pinecone. Arrange rosemary sprigs at top.
Yield: about 16 servings

Chicken-Artichoke-Cheese Spread Gift Box

Chicken-Artichoke-Cheese Spread Gift Box

This recipe can make two gifts, if you prefer. Simply cut the loaf into two small "boxes" and garnish each half.

- 3 cups diced cooked chicken
- 2 packages (8 ounces each) cream cheese, softened
- 2 cups freshly shredded Parmesan cheese
- 1 can (14 ounces) artichoke hearts, drained and diced
- 1 cup finely chopped pecans, toasted
- 4 green onions, minced
- 1 tablespoon lemon juice
- ½ teaspoon salt
- 1 teaspoon seasoned pepper
- 7 to 8 green onion stems and 1 red chile pepper, halved, to garnish

In a large bowl, combine chicken and next 8 ingredients; stir until blended. Spoon into a straight-sided 5 x 9-inch loaf pan lined with plastic wrap. Cover and chill 8 hours.

Invert chilled mixture onto a serving plate; remove plastic wrap. Cut loaf in half crosswise, place 1 cut half directly on top of remaining cut half, and smooth sides.

Garnish by plunging green onion stems into boiling water; plunge stems into ice water to stop the cooking process. Immediately transfer to paper towels; drain stems, and press between paper towels to dry. Press stems into sides of cheese square, beginning with the end of one stem on each side. Bring stems up and over to center of top; form loops with remaining stems, and secure with wooden picks. Arrange chile pepper halves on top. Cover and chill up to 4 days.

Yield: about 24 appetizer servings

Freezing 101

- Good food choices for freezing are baked cake layers, breads, cookies, shredded cheese, crumb toppings, and soups and stews.
- Never freeze cooked egg whites, aspics and gelatins, salad ingredients, cream pies, potatoes, rice, or canned goods.
- Prevent freezer burn by choosing the proper container size for the amount of food you are freezing, and tightly sealing to prevent excess air from entering the container.
- Do not refreeze cooked dishes that have already been frozen and reheated—this affects the flavor and nutrients.

Pepper-Pimiento Cheese

This four-pepper pimiento cheese packs a flavorful punch. It makes two or three gifts when presented in crocks.

- 2 blocks (8 ounces each) extra sharp Cheddar cheese, shredded
- 1 block (8 ounces) Monterey Jack cheese with jalapeño peppers, shredded
- 1 cup mayonnaise
- 1 can (4.5 ounces) chopped green chiles
- 1 jar (4 ounces) diced pimientos, drained
- 1 medium poblano chile pepper, seeded and minced
- ¼ small sweet onion, minced
- 2 teaspoons Worcestershire sauce

In a large bowl, stir together all ingredients. Cover and chill up to 4 days.

Yield: about 6 cups cheese

Peppercorn Cheese Log

Green and pink peppercorns surrounding this cheese log create a holiday essence perfect for gift giving.

- 1 can (14½ ounces) whole tomatoes, well drained and chopped
- 1 container (8 ounces) soft cream cheese
- 2 cups (8 ounces) shredded sharp Cheddar cheese
- ½ cup butter or margarine, softened
- 1 small onion, finely chopped
- 2 cloves garlic, pressed
- ½ teaspoon salt
- ⅛ to ¼ teaspoon ground black pepper
  Coarsely cracked black, green, and pink peppercorns

In a large bowl, combine tomatoes, cheeses, butter, onion, garlic, salt, and pepper; stir together. Shape into a log. Roll in coarsely cracked peppercorns. Cover and chill up to 4 days. Serve with crackers.

Yield: about 8 to 10 appetizer servings

Curry-Almond Cheese Spread

Curry-Almond Cheese Spread

An old round tin makes an ideal container for this sweetly spiced dip. Place the spread on a plate and position the plate inside a tissue paper-lined tin.

    2 packages (8 ounces each) cream cheese,
        softened
    1 jar (9 ounces) mango chutney
    1 cup slivered almonds, toasted
    1 tablespoon curry powder
    1/2 teaspoon dry mustard
        Toasted slivered almonds
        Fresh cranberries to garnish

Process cream cheese, chutney, almonds, curry powder, and mustard in a food processor until smooth, stopping to scrape down sides. Cover and chill 1 hour.

Shape mixture into a round. Chill until ready to serve or up to 4 days. Sprinkle with almonds. Garnish with cranberries.

Yield: about 3 cups spread

Herb-Butter Cheese Spread

Fill a crock with this creamy, herbed cheese spread and package it in a basket with fruit, a loaf of French bread, and a bottle of wine—an instant party!

    2 packages (16 ounces each) cream cheese,
        softened
    1 carton (8 ounces) whipped butter, softened
    2 cloves garlic, pressed
    1/2 teaspoon dried oregano leaves
    1/4 teaspoon dried basil leaves
    1/4 teaspoon dried marjoram leaves
    1/4 teaspoon dried thyme leaves
    1/4 teaspoon ground black pepper

In a mixing bowl, beat cream cheese at medium speed of an electric mixer until smooth; add butter and remaining ingredients, mixing until blended. Spoon into an airtight container. Store in refrigerator up to 4 days.

Yield: about 3½ cups spread

Quick Crackers

Friends will enjoy these thin, crisp crackers for a snack or served with a salad.

    1 package (16 ounces) egg roll wrappers
    3 tablespoons olive oil
    3 tablespoons water
    3/4 teaspoon garlic salt
    3/4 teaspoon dried Italian herb seasoning
    1/4 to 1/2 teaspoon ground red pepper
        Parmesan cheese

Cut each egg roll wrapper into 4 strips with kitchen shears. Arrange in a single layer on lightly greased baking sheets. Set aside.

Preheat oven to 375 degrees. Combine olive oil, water, garlic salt, seasoning, and red pepper. Brush mixture onto each strip.

Bake 5 to 6 minutes or until golden. Sprinkle lightly with Parmesan cheese. Remove to wire racks to cool. Store in an airtight container.

Yield: about 6 dozen crackers

Crackers

Dips and spreads can be intimidating when you don't know which cracker to pair with them. Not to worry. Here's an overview of crackers that best accompany these cheesy treats.

- Try garlic Melba toast with a thicker, flavorful spread like Buttery Blue Cheese Spread with Walnuts (page 18). It's a sturdy cracker, and its mild flavor will not overpower the spread.

- Lavash is a good choice for a mild cracker to accompany a salty spread. Pair it with Sicilian-Style Caponata (page 21) or Pepper-Pimiento Cheese (page 15).

- Wheatberry crackers are slightly sweet. They complement a tangy dip, so they're a match for Curry Dip (page 23).

- Basic corn chips or stone-ground wheat crackers are sturdy and work well for a creamy, soft dip like Cilantro Dip (page 21).

Buttery Blue Cheese Spread with Walnuts

Present this spread in a hollowed-out bread loaf for a hostess gift to serve right away. Fill the loaf just before giving it to make sure the loaf doesn't get soggy. To give the spread so that it keeps longer, spoon the spread into a crock instead of the bread loaf. Present it with toasted baguette slices and apples or pears for slicing.

    3 packages (8 ounces each) cream cheese,
        softened
    ½ cup butter, softened
    1 package (4 ounces) crumbled blue cheese
    ½ cup diced walnuts, toasted
    ½ cup chopped fresh chives
    ¼ cup cream sherry (optional)
    1 round bread loaf (16 ounces)
        Toasted diced walnuts, chopped fresh chives,
        and fresh rosemary sprigs to garnish

In a large bowl, stir together cream cheese, butter, blue cheese, walnuts, chives, and, if desired, sherry; cover and chill mixture until ready to fill bread loaf. Let stand at room temperature to soften.

Hollow out bread loaf, leaving a 1-inch-thick shell; reserve inside of loaf for other uses. Spoon softened cheese spread into shell. Garnish with walnuts, chives, and rosemary sprigs.

Yield: about 5 cups spread

Smoky Green Chile-Cheddar Cheese with Avocado-Mango Salsa

Smoked Cheddar cheese adds an earthy flavor to these Southwestern cheese rounds; find it in the deli section of your grocery store. Be sure to give these gifts with a bag of crisp tortilla chips. If the gifts won't be eaten right away, give the salsa separately in a Mason jar.

    2 packages (8 ounces each) cream cheese,
        softened
    2 blocks (8 ounces each) Monterey Jack cheese
        with peppers, shredded
   16 ounces smoked Cheddar cheese, shredded
    6 green onions, minced
    2 cans (4.5 ounces each) chopped green chiles,
        drained
    1 envelope (1¼ ounces) taco seasoning mix
        Avocado-Mango Salsa

In a large bowl, combine cheeses, onion, green chiles, and seasoning mix. Divide mixture into 2 equal portions; shape each into a 6-inch round. Cover and chill 8 hours.

Place cheese rounds on gift plates; top evenly with Avocado-Mango Salsa.

Yield: about 18 appetizer servings

Avocado-Mango Salsa

    ¼ cup hot jalapeño jelly
    ¼ cup freshly squeezed lime juice
    2 large mangoes, peeled and diced
    2 large avocados, diced
    1 large sweet red pepper, diced
    ¼ cup chopped fresh cilantro

In a large bowl, whisk together jelly and lime juice. Add remaining ingredients, and stir until blended. Cover and chill at least 2 hours or up to 24 hours.

Yield: about 5 cups salsa

Note: Substitute 1 jar (26 ounces) refrigerated mango pieces, drained, for fresh mango, if desired.

Buttery Blue Cheese Spread with Walnuts and Smoky Green Chile-Cheddar Cheese with Avocado-Mango Salsa

Cheese Terrine

This tricolor terrine makes a festive appetizer gift dressed up for a holiday celebration. Present the terrine with the marinara sauce and Italian bread for serving.

- ¼ cup dry white wine
- 1 pound provolone cheese, cut into ¹⁄₁₆-inch-thick slices
- Pesto Filling
- Walnut-Goat Cheese Filling
- Sun-Dried Tomato Filling
- 1 jar (15 ounces) marinara sauce
- Italian bread
- Fresh basil leaves and walnut halves to garnish

Cut a single piece of cheesecloth to fit into a 4-cup ring mold; dampen with wine, gently squeezing out excess moisture. Line mold with cheesecloth, allowing excess to extend over rim.

Cut provolone cheese slices in half. Line bottom and sides of mold with half of cheese slices. Divide remaining cheese into 3 equal portions; set aside.

Spoon Pesto Filling over cheese in ring mold. Top with one-third of remaining cheese slices. Spoon Walnut-Goat Cheese Filling over cheese slices; layer another one-third of cheese slices on top. Spoon Sun-Dried Tomato Filling over cheese slices, spreading gently to edges; top with remaining cheese slices. Fold cheesecloth over top, and press lightly. Cover and chill at least 8 hours or up to 2 days.

Unfold cheesecloth, and invert terrine onto a gift platter. Discard cheesecloth.

Yield: about 16 appetizer servings

Directions for gift card: To serve, cut terrine into 1-inch slices. Serve with marinara sauce on Italian bread slices. Garnish with basil leaves and walnut halves.

Cheese Terrine

Pesto Filling

    1 cup firmly packed fresh basil leaves
    1 cup freshly grated Parmesan cheese
    ½ cup olive oil
    2 cloves garlic, sliced

In container of an electric blender, combine basil, cheese, oil, and garlic. Cover and process until almost smooth, scraping down sides of container occasionally.
Yield: about 1 cup filling

Walnut-Goat Cheese Filling

    1 cup crumbled goat cheese
    ⅔ cup chopped walnuts, toasted
    ¼ cup sour cream
    1 clove garlic, sliced

In container of an electric blender, combine cheese, walnuts, sour cream, and garlic. Cover and process until almost smooth, scraping down sides of container occasionally.
Yield: about 1¼ cups filling

Sun-Dried Tomato Filling

    1 jar (7 ounces) oil-packed sun-dried tomatoes, undrained
    1 cup freshly grated Parmesan cheese
    2 teaspoons lemon juice

In container of an electric blender, combine tomatoes, cheese, and lemon juice. Cover and process until almost smooth, scraping sides of container occasionally.
Yield: about 1¼ cups filling

Raw Veggies

Raw vegetables are great make-ahead dippers and are easy to transport. Simply place the washed veggies in a resealable plastic bag or plastic storage container alongside your gift of spread or dip, and you're on your way. Be sure to refrigerate your prepared vegetables to retain freshness until you're ready to deliver the package.

Ideal vegetable choices are listed below.

- Carrot sticks
- Celery sticks
- Cherry or grape tomatoes
- Yellow squash slices
- Zucchini slices
- Broccoli flowerets
- Cauliflower flowerets

Cilantro Dip

(pictured on page 6)

This pretty pale green dip is ideal for a Southwestern style holiday celebration. Give it with raw vegetables or holiday-colored tortilla chips.

    1 package (6 ounces) feta cheese
    1 cup milk
    1 package (8 ounces) cream cheese
    1 can (8 ounces) green Mexican sauce
    ¼ cup chopped fresh cilantro
    1 clove garlic

Cut feta into 1-inch pieces. Place in a bowl; add milk. Cover and chill 8 hours. (Soaking reduces the sodium content.) Drain and discard milk.
In a food processor, process feta cheese, cream cheese, Mexican sauce, cilantro, and garlic until smooth, stopping to scrape down sides. Chill at least 30 minutes or up to 1 week.
Yield: about 1¼ cups dip

Sicilian-Style Caponata

Introduce friends to this tangy Sicilian relish that can be served warm or chilled. Give it with a loaf of rustic bread to serve alongside.

    2 medium eggplants
    ½ cup olive oil
    2 small onions, diced
    3 tablespoons tomato sauce
    2 ribs celery, diced
    ¼ cup capers
    6 pitted green olives, chopped
    6 pitted black olives, chopped
    2 tablespoons sugar
    2 tablespoons white vinegar
    ½ teaspoon salt
    ½ teaspoon ground black pepper

Peel and dice eggplants. Sauté in hot oil in a Dutch oven over medium-high heat 5 minutes; remove eggplant from pan, and set aside.
Add onion to pan; sauté 5 minutes or until tender. Add tomato sauce and celery; sauté 5 minutes or until celery is tender.
Return eggplant to pan; stir in capers and next 6 ingredients. Reduce heat, and simmer, stirring often, 20 minutes. Cool 1 hour. Cover and chill up to 1 week.
Yield: about 5 cups caponata

Pumpkin Pie Dip

Pumpkin Pie Dip Quick & Easy

Give this sweet dip in a simple reusable container along with gingersnaps and pears or apples for slicing.

  1 package (8 ounces) cream cheese, softened
  2 cups confectioners sugar
  1 can (15 ounces) pumpkin
  1 teaspoon ground cinnamon
 ½ teaspoon ground ginger

Beat cream cheese and sugar at medium speed of an electric mixer until smooth. Add pumpkin, cinnamon, and ginger, beating well. Cover and chill up to 5 days.
Yield: about 3 cups dip

Red Pepper Hummus

Share this hummus with a bag of pita chips for a ready-to-serve gift.

   1 large sweet red pepper
   1 can (15 ounces) chickpeas, rinsed and drained
   1 clove garlic
  ¼ cup lemon juice
   3 tablespoons tahini
   2 tablespoons olive oil
   2 tablespoons fresh parsley
   1 tablespoon lite soy sauce
1½ teaspoons ground cumin
  ½ teaspoon ground red pepper
  ⅛ teaspoon salt

Cut peppers in half lengthwise; remove and discard seeds and membranes. Place peppers, skin side up, on a large baking sheet; flatten peppers with palm of hand. Broil 5½ inches from heat 15 to 20 minutes or until charred. Place peppers in ice water until cool. Remove from water; peel and discard skins.

In a food processor, process sweet pepper and remaining ingredients until smooth, stopping to scrape down sides. Cover and chill up to 5 days.
Yield: about 2 cups hummus

Curry Dip Quick & Easy

Package this dip with an assortment of raw vegetables for a no-fuss appetizer gift.

  1 container (8 ounces) sour cream
 ½ cup mayonnaise
  2 tablespoons minced fresh parsley
  1 tablespoon minced fresh chives
  2 tablespoons grated onion
  2 tablespoons lemon juice
  1 teaspoon curry powder
  2 teaspoons prepared mustard
 ½ teaspoon salt
 ½ teaspoon paprika
 ½ teaspoon dried tarragon leaves

In a medium bowl, stir together all ingredients. Cover and chill at least 4 hours or up to 1 week.
Yield: about 1½ cups dip

Red Pepper Hummus

Roasted Garlic and Pepper Dip

Garlic mellows as it roasts, and two heads of roasted garlic provide robust flavor to this red pepper dip. Bundle it alongside breadsticks, pita chips, or veggies for dipping.

- 2 large heads garlic
- 2 large sweet red peppers
- 1 cup cottage cheese
- 2 ounces goat cheese
- ¼ cup sour cream
- ½ teaspoon hot sauce

Preheat oven to 350 degrees. Peel outer skin from each garlic head, and discard. Cut off top one-third of each garlic head. Place garlic, cut side up, in center of a piece of heavy-duty aluminum foil. Fold foil over garlic, sealing tightly. Bake 1 hour or until garlic is soft. Remove from oven; cool 10 minutes. Remove and discard papery skin from garlic. Squeeze pulp from each clove, or scoop out with a spoon; set pulp aside.

Cut peppers in half lengthwise; remove and discard seeds and membranes. Place peppers, skin side up, on a large baking sheet; flatten peppers with palm of hand. Broil 5½ inches from heat 15 to 20 minutes or until charred. Place peppers in ice water until cool. Remove from water; peel and discard skins.

Combine garlic pulp, peppers, cottage cheese, and remaining ingredients in container of an electric blender; cover and process until smooth, stopping once to scrape down sides. Spoon mixture into a small bowl; cover and chill at least 2 hours.
Yield: about 2¼ cups dip

Rosy Red Wine Vinaigrette

Funnel this vinaigrette into giftable cruets and pair with prepackaged salad greens and breadsticks or croutons.

- 2 fresh rosemary sprigs (6 inches each)
- 1⅓ cups red wine vinegar
- 2 cups olive oil
- 1 clove garlic, finely chopped
- 1 tablespoon Dijon mustard
- ½ teaspoon salt
- ¼ teaspoon ground white pepper

Place rosemary in a 1-quart jar. Bring vinegar to a boil; pour hot vinegar into jar. Cover and let stand at room temperature overnight. Remove and discard rosemary.

Add oil and remaining ingredients to vinegar in jar. Cover tightly and shake vigorously. Cover and chill.
Yield: about 3¾ cups vinaigrette

Directions for gift card: Store in refrigerator up to 1 week. Shake before serving over salad greens or steamed or raw veggies.

Pickled Vegetables

Pickled vegetables are so pretty you won't want to wrap them. Just cover the lid with a square of handmade paper and tie with a gold ribbon.

- 1 large head cauliflower
- 2 quarts water
- 1 quart white vinegar
- ¾ cup honey
- 3 tablespoons mustard seed
- 1½ teaspoons celery seed
- ½ teaspoon black peppercorns
- 1 pound baby carrots, scraped
- 6 ribs celery, cut into 2-inch strips
- 1 medium-size green pepper, cut into 1½-inch strips
- 1 medium-size sweet red pepper, cut into 1½-inch strips
- 1 can (16 ounces) whole green beans, drained
- 8 small cloves garlic
- 8 small hot peppers
- 1 teaspoon salt

Remove large outer leaves of cauliflower; break into flowerets. Set aside.

In a non-aluminum Dutch oven, combine water, vinegar, honey, mustard seed, celery seed, and peppercorns. Bring to a boil; reduce heat, and simmer 30 minutes.

Remove foam from surface. Add carrots. Bring to a boil; reduce heat, and simmer 3 minutes. Add cauliflower and celery. Bring to a boil; reduce heat, and simmer 5 minutes.

Add pepper strips and beans, and simmer 3 minutes.

Spoon vegetables into 8 (2-cup) containers. Pour hot vinegar mixture over vegetables, evenly distributing spices.

Add 1 clove garlic, 1 hot pepper, and ⅛ teaspoon salt to each container. Cool.

Seal containers, and refrigerate 1 week.
Yield: 8 (2-cup) gifts

Directions for gift card: Store Pickled Vegetables in refrigerator up to 3 weeks.

Pickled Vegetables

Zesty Cheese and Olives

The zesty flavors of this appetizer intensify as the mixture soaks. Tie a decorative ornament to each jar to make four gifts from this recipe.

> 10 cloves garlic, cut in half
> 3 cups olive oil, divided
> 1 cup white wine vinegar
> ¼ cup Dijon mustard
> ¼ cup lemon juice
> 2 tablespoons dried oregano leaves
> 2 teaspoons cracked black pepper
> 1 teaspoon salt
> 1 teaspoon dried crushed red pepper
> 2 jars (7 ounces each) Sicilian olives, drained
> 2 packages (8 ounces each) Cheddar cheese,
>   cut into ¾-inch cubes
> 2 cups kalamata olives
> 2 packages (8 ounces each) mozzarella cheese,
>   cut into ¾-inch cubes

In a medium saucepan, cook garlic in ½ cup oil over medium-high heat, stirring constantly, until golden. Remove from heat, and cool. Add remaining 2½ cups oil, vinegar, mustard, lemon juice, oregano, black pepper, salt, and red pepper; stir well with a wire whisk.

Layer Sicilian olives and remaining ingredients evenly in 4 (1-quart) jars. Pour marinade over layers; cover tightly, and marinate in refrigerator at least 2 days.
Yield: 4 (1-quart) jars

Directions for gift card: Store in refrigerator up to 2 weeks. The longer the cheese is stored, the firmer it becomes. Drain before serving; serve at room temperature.

Lemon-Basil Vegetables

The palate-pleasing combination of lemon and basil makes these vegetables suitable to give as an appetizer or salad. Tie an antique serving fork from a flea market to the bottle for a personal touch.

> 7 cups fresh broccoli flowerets (about 1 pound)
> 1 package (8 ounces) small fresh mushrooms
> 1 large sweet red pepper, cut into thin strips
> 1 small red onion, thinly sliced
>   Zest of 1 lemon, cut into strips
> 1¼ cups vegetable oil
> ½ cup fresh lemon juice
> 2 teaspoons dried basil leaves
> 1 teaspoon garlic salt
> ¼ teaspoon ground black pepper

In a large shallow container, combine broccoli, mushrooms, pepper, onion, and lemon zest; toss gently.

Combine oil and remaining ingredients in a small bowl, stirring with a wire whisk.

Pour marinade over vegetables; toss gently to coat. Cover and marinate in refrigerator at least 8 hours, tossing occasionally.
Yield: about 20 servings

Directions for gift card: Store in refrigerator up to 4 days. Drain before serving. Serve as antipasto vegetables on a relish tray or as a marinated salad.

Greek Vegetable Salsa

Traditional Greek flavors breathe new identity into this tomato salsa that your friends can relish over grilled flank steak or fish, or enjoy as a dip for pita wedges.

> 1 pound tomatoes, diced
> ½ cup diced cucumber
> ¼ cup chopped red onion
> 1 can (2¼ ounces) sliced ripe olives
> 2 tablespoons chopped fresh parsley
> 2 tablespoons lemon juice
> 1 tablespoon olive oil
> 1 clove garlic, minced
> ½ teaspoon chopped dried rosemary leaves
> ⅛ teaspoon salt
> ⅛ teaspoon ground black pepper
> ½ cup crumbled feta cheese

In a medium bowl, stir together tomatoes, cucumber, onion, olives, and parsley. Whisk together lemon juice, oil, garlic, rosemary, salt, and pepper. Toss together tomato mixture and oil mixture; sprinkle with feta cheese.
Yield: about 2½ cups salsa

Mexican Mocha Spice Mix

Mexican Mocha Spice Mix

Tuck a heavy-duty resealable plastic bag of this mix into a decorative fabric bag for a thoughtful gift. Include a bag of miniature marshmallows to carry out the cozy theme. You can also use this spice blend to flavor angel food cake (see page 144).

    1 cup cocoa
    1 cup sugar
    ½ cup non-dairy powdered creamer
    2 tablespoons instant coffee granules
    1 teaspoon ground cinnamon
    ½ teaspoon ground nutmeg

In a large heavy-duty resealable plastic bag, combine all ingredients; seal and shake to blend. Store in an airtight container.
Yield: about 2½ cups mix

Directions for gift card: To serve, spoon ¼ cup mixture into coffee mug, and stir in 1 cup hot water.
Yield: about 20 servings

Spiced Tea Punch Mix

Place this mix in a decorative gift canister for convenient use anytime.

>   1 jar (21.1 ounces) orange-flavored
>   powdered instant breakfast drink mix
>   ¾ cup lemon-flavored powdered instant tea mix
>   1½ cups sugar
>   1½ teaspoons ground cloves
>   1½ teaspoons ground cinnamon

In a large bowl, combine drink mix, instant tea mix, sugar, cloves, and cinnamon. Store in an airtight container.
Yield: about 5 cups mix

Directions for gift card: In a Dutch oven, bring ¾ cup Spiced Tea Punch Mix, 1 can (46 ounces) unsweetened pineapple juice, 1 can (46 ounces) apple juice, and 2 cups water to a boil; reduce heat, and simmer, stirring occasionally, 15 minutes. Serve hot or cold.
Yield: about 13 cups punch per ¾ cup mix

Quick and easy option: To make a simple single serving, combine 1½ tablespoons mix with 1 cup boiling water. Serve hot or cold.

Mulled Cranberry Cider

The recipient of this gift will be excited to start the holiday celebration with this warming cider. Save old wine bottles to use as gift packaging, and drizzle colored hot wax over the corks for a cheery presentation.

>   8 black peppercorns
>   6 whole allspice
>   6 whole cloves
>   2 cinnamon sticks (3 inches each)
>   1 gallon apple cider
>   2 quarts cranberry juice cocktail

Place peppercorns, allspice, cloves, and cinnamon sticks on a 5-inch-square piece of cheesecloth; tie with string.
In a Dutch oven, bring cider and juice to a boil with spice bag. Partially cover, reduce heat, and simmer 30 minutes. Remove and discard spice bag before serving. Serve hot or cold.
Yield: about 1½ gallons cider

Directions for gift card: Store in refrigerator up to a week; serve hot or cold.

Coffee Liqueur

This liqueur makes a perfect match for eggnog. Package it in a decorative bottle for friends to nip in their 'nog.

>   1½ cups sugar
>   1 cup firmly packed dark brown sugar
>   2 cups water
>   ½ cup instant coffee granules
>   3 cups vodka
>   ¼ cup whole coffee beans

In a medium saucepan, combine sugar, brown sugar, and water. Cook over medium-high heat until mixture comes to a boil; reduce heat, and simmer 5 minutes. Remove from heat, and stir in coffee granules. Cool. Combine coffee mixture, vodka, and coffee beans; pour into a 1-gallon jar. Cover tightly, and store in a dark place at room temperature at least 2 weeks. Shake jar gently once daily.
Pour mixture through a wire-mesh strainer lined with 2 layers of cheesecloth into jars, discarding coffee beans. Cover tightly. Store at room temperature.
Yield: about 6 cups liqueur

Directions for gift card: Store at room temperature. Use in beverages, eggnog, flavored cheesecakes, or cake fillings and batters.

Raspberry Cordial

This sweet raspberry-laced liqueur may be used in a number of ways. Give it in a pretty bottle along with a copy of your favorite recipe for flavored coffee or trifle.

>   2 packages (10 ounces each) frozen raspberries
>   in light syrup, thawed
>   1¾ cups sugar
>   ¾ cup water
>   3½ cups brandy

In a medium saucepan, combine raspberries, sugar, and water; cook over medium-high heat until mixture comes to a boil; reduce heat, and simmer 5 minutes. Remove from heat, and cool. Pour into a 1-gallon jar. Add brandy, and stir well. Cover tightly, and store in refrigerator at least 2 weeks. Shake jar gently once daily.
Pour mixture through a wire-mesh strainer lined with 2 layers of cheesecloth into jars, discarding raspberries. Cover tightly. Store at room temperature.
Yield: about 4¾ cups liqueur

Directions for gift card: Store at room temperature. Use in beverages, trifles, or sauces.

Praline Liqueur

Make Ahead

Here's a great gift for the pecan lover on your list.

>   2 cups firmly packed dark brown sugar
>   1 cup sugar
>   2½ cups water
>   4 cups pecan pieces, lightly toasted
>   2 vanilla beans, split lengthwise
>   4 cups vodka

In a saucepan, combine brown sugar, sugar, and water. Cook over medium-high heat until mixture comes to a boil; reduce heat, and simmer 5 minutes.

Place pecans and vanilla beans in a 1-gallon jar. Pour hot mixture into jar, and cool. Add vodka, and stir well. Cover tightly, and store in a dark place at room temperature at least 2 weeks. Shake jar gently once daily.

Pour mixture through a wire-mesh strainer lined with 2 layers of cheesecloth into a bowl, discarding solids. Pour mixture through a wire-mesh strainer lined with a coffee filter into a bowl. Change filter often. (Mixture will drip slowly.) Pour mixture into jars; cover tightly. Store at room temperature.
Yield: about 4½ cups liqueur

Directions for gift card: Store at room temperature. Use in coffee, baked apples, or flavored cheesecakes.

Coffee Liqueur, Raspberry Cordial, and Praline Liqueur

Butter Rolls, page 52;
Gingerbread Muffins, page 37

Santa's Breadshoppe

Breads warm the heart and
soul in this cool season.
Whether for breakfast, lunch,
or dinner, they comfort
everyone and complete any
meal. Packaged with a
decorative ornament, these
breads will be welcome gifts.

Bacon-and-Cheese Biscuits

Place these savory biscuits in a caddy lined with decorative tissue paper for a ready-to-nibble gift.

- 1½ cups all-purpose flour
- 2½ teaspoons baking powder
- ¼ teaspoon salt
- ½ cup vegetable shortening
- 12 slices bacon, cooked and crumbled
- 1 cup (4 ounces) shredded sharp Cheddar cheese
- ¼ cup chopped onion
- ½ cup milk

Preheat oven to 425 degrees. In a large bowl, stir together flour, baking powder, and salt. With a pastry blender, cut in shortening until crumbly; stir in bacon, cheese, and onion. Add milk, stirring just until dry ingredients are moistened.

Turn dough out onto a lightly floured surface; knead 4 or 5 times.

Roll dough into an 8 x 9-inch rectangle; cut into 1 x 3-inch rectangles, and place on a lightly greased baking sheet.

Bake 12 minutes or until lightly browned.
Yield: about 2 dozen biscuits

Bacon-and-Cheese Biscuits

Lemon Drop Biscuits

These luscious lemon biscuits make a sweet but lowfat breakfast nibble or snack—perfect for someone with a sweet tooth but watching what they eat.

    3½ cups low-fat biscuit & baking mix
    ¼ cup lemonade drink mix
    ½ cup currants
    2 teaspoons grated lemon zest
    1⅔ cups fat-free milk
        Lemon Glaze

Preheat oven to 425 degrees. In a large bowl, combine baking mix, drink mix, currants, and lemon zest; add milk, stirring just until dry ingredients are moistened.

Drop dough by rounded tablespoonfuls onto lightly greased baking sheets.

Bake 10 minutes or until golden. Drizzle biscuits evenly with Lemon Glaze.
Yield: about 22 biscuits

Lemon Glaze

    1½ cups confectioners sugar
    2 tablespoons fresh lemon juice

Stir together sugar and lemon juice.
Yield: about ⅔ cup glaze

Sweet Potato Biscuits  Big Batch

Give someone the gift of enjoying sweet potatoes in a new way. Leftover holiday ham tucked in the center of these sweet, flaky biscuits will delight all ages.

    1 envelope (¼ ounce) dry yeast
    ¼ cup warm water (100 degrees to
         110 degrees)
    1 can (15 ounces) sweet potatoes in syrup,
         drained and mashed
    ½ cup butter or margarine, softened
    ½ cup sugar
    1 teaspoon salt
    2½ cups all-purpose flour
    1 teaspoon baking powder
        Melted butter

In a glass measuring cup, combine yeast and ¼ cup warm water; let stand 5 minutes.

Stir together sweet potatoes and butter, blending well. Stir in sugar and salt; add yeast mixture, stirring until smooth.

Combine flour and baking powder; gradually stir into potato mixture until well blended. Lightly knead until dough holds together.

Shape dough into a ball; place in a buttered mixing bowl. Brush top with melted butter. Cover and let rise in a warm place (85 degrees), free from drafts, 2½ hours or until doubled in size.

Punch dough down, and turn out onto a floured surface. Roll dough to ½-inch thickness; cut with a 2-inch round cutter, and place on greased baking sheets. Cover and let rise in a warm place, free from drafts, 2 hours or until doubled in size.

Preheat oven to 400 degrees. Bake 12 minutes or until golden.
Yield: about 34 biscuits

Ginger Scones

(pictured on page 95)

Crystallized ginger gives these scones a refreshing flavor snap—an intriguing addition to any gift basket.

    2¾ cups all-purpose flour
    2 teaspoons baking powder
    ½ teaspoon salt
    ½ cup sugar
    ¾ cup cold butter
    ⅓ cup chopped crystallized ginger
    1 cup milk

Preheat oven to 400 degrees. In a large bowl, combine flour, baking powder, salt, and sugar. With a pastry blender, cut butter into flour mixture until crumbly. Stir in ginger. Add milk, stirring just until dry ingredients are moistened.

Turn dough out onto a lightly floured surface, and knead 10 to 15 times. Pat or roll dough to ¾-inch thickness; shape into a round, and cut dough into 8 wedges. Place wedges on a lightly greased baking sheet.

Bake 16 to 18 minutes or until barely golden. Cool slightly on a wire rack. Serve warm.
Yield: 8 scones

Hot Raisin Scones

Hot Raisin Scones

The ingredients in these scones are simple and inexpensive, and the results are impressively tasty. Wrap them up for a favorite aunt, along with a pretty tin of flavored tea.

- 2 cups all-purpose flour
- 2 teaspoons baking powder
- ½ teaspoon baking soda
- ¼ teaspoon salt
- 2 tablespoons sugar
- 1 teaspoon grated lemon zest
- ½ cup cold butter or margarine
- ½ cup raisins
- ¾ cup buttermilk

Preheat oven to 425 degrees. In a large bowl, combine flour, baking powder, baking soda, salt, sugar, and lemon zest. With a pastry blender, cut in butter until mixture is crumbly. Add raisins, tossing lightly. Add buttermilk, stirring until dry ingredients are moistened.

Turn dough out onto a lightly floured surface, and knead lightly 6 times. Divide dough in half. Shape each portion into a 7-inch circle on an ungreased baking sheet; cut each circle into 6 wedges.

Bake 10 minutes. Cool on wire racks.

Place scones on 2 (8-inch) cake boards; wrap with heavy-duty plastic wrap.

Yield: 1 dozen scones

Directions for gift card: Freeze scones up to 1 month, if desired. Thaw at room temperature; bake at 425 degrees for 6 to 7 minutes or until thoroughly heated.

Cinnamon Breakfast Puffs

These sweet little muffins taste like cinnamon bread. Tuck them in a basket with a bag of freshly ground coffee for a memorable morning.

- ⅓ cup butter, softened
- ½ cup sugar
- 1 egg
- 1½ cups all-purpose flour
- 1½ teaspoons baking powder
- ½ teaspoon salt
- ¼ teaspoon ground nutmeg
- ½ cup milk
- ½ cup sugar
- 1 teaspoon ground cinnamon
- 6 tablespoons butter, melted

Preheat oven to 400 degrees. Beat ⅓ cup butter at medium speed of an electric mixer until creamy. Gradually add ½ cup sugar, beating well. Add egg, beating mixture well.

Combine flour, baking powder, salt, and nutmeg; add to butter mixture alternately with milk, beginning and ending with flour mixture. Mix at low speed after each addition until blended.

Place paper muffin cups in muffin pans, and coat with cooking spray; spoon batter into cups, filling two-thirds full.

Bake 14 to 15 minutes or until golden. Remove muffins from pan.

Combine ½ cup sugar and cinnamon in a bowl; stir well. Dip tops of muffins into melted butter; roll buttered tops in cinnamon mixture.

Yield: about 1 dozen muffins

Date-Nut Bran Muffins

You can have a hearty homemade gift in minutes with these muffins that start with a mix.

- 1 package (7 ounces) bran muffin mix
- ½ cup chopped dates
- ½ cup coarsely chopped pecans
- 1 tablespoon brown sugar
- Dash of ground cinnamon
- 1 egg
- ½ cup milk

Preheat oven to 425 degrees. In a large bowl, combine muffin mix, dates, pecans, sugar, and cinnamon; make a well in center of mixture. Set aside.

Combine egg and milk; add to dry ingredients, stirring just until moistened.

Spoon into greased or paper-lined muffin pans, filling three-fourths full.

Bake 12 minutes or until golden. Remove from pans immediately.

Yield: about 9 muffins

Squash-Corn Muffins

Squash-Corn Muffins

Flecks of sweet red pepper and a dash of chili powder give these tender corn muffins a Southwestern flair.

　1¼　cups all-purpose flour
　¾　cup yellow cornmeal
　2　teaspoons baking soda
　¼　teaspoon salt
　2½　teaspoons brown sugar
　1　teaspoon chili powder
　1¼　cups buttermilk
　2½　tablespoons olive oil
　1　egg, lightly beaten
　¾　cup shredded yellow squash (about 1 small)
　¼　cup frozen whole-kernel corn, thawed
　¼　cup diced sweet red pepper

Preheat oven to 400 degrees. In a medium bowl, combine flour, cornmeal, baking soda, salt, brown sugar, and chili powder; make a well in center of mixture.

Combine buttermilk, oil, and egg; add to dry ingredients, stirring just until moistened. Gently stir in squash, corn, and red pepper. Spoon batter into muffin pans coated with cooking spray, filling three-fourths full.

Bake 15 minutes or until golden. Remove from pans immediately.

Yield: about 1 dozen muffins

Peanut Butter Muffins

Pack these streusel-topped muffins with a jar of homemade jelly for a PB&J treat.

　2　cups all-purpose flour
　½　cup sugar
　2　teaspoons baking powder
　1　teaspoon salt
　¾　cup creamy or crunchy peanut butter
　1　egg
　1　cup milk
　½　cup uncooked regular oats
　2　tablespoons golden raisins, chopped
　2　tablespoons honey
　1　tablespoon butter or margarine, melted

Preheat oven to 350 degrees. In a medium bowl, combine flour, sugar, baking powder, and salt. With a fork or pastry blender, cut in peanut butter until crumbly.

Stir together egg and milk; stir into dry ingredients just until moistened. Pour batter into greased muffin pans, filling two-thirds full.

Stir together oats, raisins, honey, and butter. Spoon mixture evenly over batter.

Bake 25 to 30 minutes. Remove muffins from pans immediately.

Yield: about 1 dozen muffins

Gingerbread Muffins

(pictured on page 30)

Nothing says the holidays like gingerbread, and the addition of real molasses in this recipe will win hearts. Slip the muffins into a new muffin pan after they have cooled, and package them with a copy of the recipe attached.

　1　cup vegetable shortening
　1　cup sugar
　1　cup molasses
　3　eggs
　1　cup buttermilk
　3　cups all-purpose flour
　1　teaspoon baking soda
　½　teaspoon salt
　1½　tablespoons ground ginger
　1　teaspoon ground cinnamon
　½　teaspoon ground nutmeg

Preheat oven to 350 degrees. Beat shortening at medium speed of an electric mixer until creamy; gradually add sugar, beating until fluffy. Add molasses; beat until blended. Add eggs, 1 at a time, beating until blended after each addition. Add buttermilk; beat until blended.

Combine flour, baking soda, salt, ginger, cinnamon, and nutmeg. Gradually add to buttermilk mixture; beat until blended.

Spoon into greased muffin pans, filling half full.

Bake 22 minutes. Remove from pans immediately.

Yield: about 2½ dozen muffins

Blueberry Streusel Muffins

You can substitute sweetened dried cranberries for the blueberries if you'd like a more seasonal muffin. Either way, the pecan streusel on top makes a merry crunch.

     1/4 cup pecan pieces
     1/4 cup firmly packed brown sugar
      3 tablespoons all-purpose flour, divided
      2 tablespoons butter or margarine
     1/2 cup uncooked regular oats
      2 cups all-purpose flour
     1/2 cup sugar
      2 teaspoons baking powder
     1/4 teaspoon baking soda
     1/4 teaspoon salt
      2 teaspoons grated lemon zest
     3/4 cup buttermilk
     1/4 cup vegetable oil
      1 egg
   1 1/2 cups fresh or frozen blueberries

Preheat oven to 400 degrees. Pulse pecans 2 or 3 times in a blender or food processor until chopped. Add brown sugar and 1 tablespoon flour; process 5 seconds. Add butter; pulse 5 or 6 times or until mixture is crumbly. Stir in oats; set aside.

Combine 2 cups flour and next 5 ingredients in a large bowl; make a well in center of mixture.

Whisk together buttermilk, oil, and egg; add to flour mixture, stirring just until moistened.

Toss blueberries with remaining 2 tablespoons flour; gently fold into batter. Spoon batter into greased muffin pans, filling two-thirds full; sprinkle batter with oat mixture.

Bake 15 to 20 minutes or until golden brown. Remove muffins immediately from pans, and cool on wire racks.

Yield: about 1 dozen muffins

Almond Streusel Muffins

Invite a friend over for coffee and these crunchy streusel-topped muffins. Then send her off with a take-home batch.

      2 cups all-purpose flour
      2 teaspoons baking powder
     1/4 teaspoon baking soda
     1/4 teaspoon salt
     1/2 cup sugar
      2 teaspoons grated lemon zest
      1 egg, lightly beaten
     3/4 cup plus 1 tablespoon buttermilk
      3 tablespoons vegetable oil
        Almond Streusel Topping

Preheat oven to 400 degrees. In a medium bowl, combine flour, baking powder, baking soda, salt, sugar, and lemon zest; make a well in center of mixture. Combine egg, buttermilk, and oil; add to dry ingredients, stirring just until dry ingredients are moistened.

Spoon batter into muffin pans coated with cooking spray, filling two-thirds full. Sprinkle evenly with Almond Streusel Topping.

Bake 15 minutes or until golden. Remove from pans immediately.

Yield: about 1 dozen muffins

Almond Streusel Topping

      6 tablespoons brown sugar
      2 tablespoons all-purpose flour
     1/2 teaspoon ground allspice
   2 1/2 tablespoons butter
      6 tablespoons uncooked regular oats
      1 tablespoon sliced almonds
     1/2 tablespoon grated lemon zest

Position knife blade in food processor bowl. Add brown sugar, flour, and allspice; pulse 2 or 3 times or until mixed. Add butter, and pulse 5 times or until mixture resembles coarse meal. Transfer to a small bowl, and stir in oats, almonds, and lemon zest.

Yield: about 1 cup topping

Almond Streusel Muffins

Vanilla Cream-Filled Éclairs

Vanilla Cream-Filled Éclairs

Choux paste is the French name for this tender pastry; we've simplified it by using pie crust mix. Place the dainty éclairs in a long shallow box trimmed with ribbon.

1⅓ cups water
1 package (11 ounces) pie crust mix
3 eggs
2 egg whites
Vanilla Pastry Cream
Chocolate Glaze

Preheat oven to 425 degrees. Bring 1⅓ cups water to a boil in a 3-quart saucepan over medium-high heat. Stir in pie crust mix, beating vigorously with a wooden spoon 1 minute or until mixture leaves sides of pan.

Place dough in bowl of a heavy-duty electric stand mixer; cool 5 minutes. Beat dough at medium speed of an electric mixer using paddle attachment. Add eggs and egg whites, 1 at a time, beating until blended after each addition. (If desired, eggs and egg whites may be added 1 at a time and beaten vigorously with a wooden spoon instead of using the mixer.)

Spoon dough into a large heavy-duty resealable plastic bag. Cut a 1½-inch opening across one corner of the bag. Pipe 4-inch-long strips of dough 2 inches apart onto ungreased baking sheets.

Bake 20 to 25 minutes or until puffed and golden. Remove from oven, and cut a small slit in side of each éclair to allow steam to escape. Cool on wire racks.

Split éclairs using a serrated knife, starting at one long side without cutting through opposite side. Pull out and discard soft dough inside.

Carefully spoon about ¼ cup Vanilla Pastry Cream into each éclair; close top of each éclair over filling. Top evenly with Chocolate Glaze. Chill éclairs for 2 hours or freeze up to 1 month.
Yield: about 1 dozen éclairs

Vanilla Pastry Cream

2 eggs
2 egg yolks
½ cup sugar
⅓ cup cornstarch
2 cups half and half
2 tablespoons butter, softened
2 teaspoons vanilla extract

In a 3-quart saucepan, whisk together eggs, yolks, sugar, and cornstarch. Gradually whisk in half and half. Cook over medium heat, whisking constantly, until mixture comes to a boil. Cook 1 minute or until mixture is thickened and bubbly. Remove from heat; whisk in butter and vanilla. Cover and chill 4 hours.
Yield: about 3 cups cream

Chocolate Glaze

1 cup semisweet chocolate morsels
¼ cup whipping cream
2 tablespoons butter, softened

Microwave morsels and whipping cream on high power (100%) in a 2-cup glass measuring cup 30 seconds to 1 minute or until melted, stirring twice. Whisk in butter until blended, and spoon immediately over éclairs.
Yield: about 1⅓ cups glaze

Eggnog Pancake Mix

Give this ready-to-enjoy pancake mix to the busy mom on your holiday gift list. It's easy to stir up using 3 ingredients.

1⅓ cups all-purpose flour
1 teaspoon baking soda
½ teaspoon salt
¼ teaspoon ground nutmeg
⅛ teaspoon ground cloves
¼ cup sugar

In a medium bowl, combine all ingredients, stirring until blended. Spoon mix into a resealable plastic bag; remove air, and seal.
Yield: enough mix for about 12 pancakes (4 inches each)

Directions for gift card: Combine Eggnog Pancake Mix, 1½ cups refrigerated eggnog, 1 egg, and 1 tablespoon vegetable oil, stirring just until moistened. Pour ¼ cup batter for each pancake onto a hot, lightly greased griddle. Cook until top is covered with bubbles and edges look cooked; turn and cook other side. Serve with butter and confectioners sugar, if desired.

Hearty Cornmeal Pancake Mix

Quick & Easy
Pack & Ship

Attach a nice pancake turner to a container of this easy pancake mix.

- 1 cup all-purpose flour
- 3 tablespoons yellow cornmeal
- 2 tablespoons brown sugar
- 1 tablespoon baking powder
- ½ teaspoon baking soda
- ½ teaspoon salt

In a medium bowl, combine all ingredients, stirring until blended. Spoon mix into a heavy-duty resealable plastic bag; remove air, and seal.
Yield: about 1½ cups mix

Directions for gift card: Add 1 egg, 1 cup buttermilk, and 1 tablespoon vegetable oil to pancake mix. Beat, using a wire whisk, until blended. Pour ¼ cup batter for each pancake onto a hot, lightly greased griddle. Cook until top is covered with bubbles and edges look cooked; turn and cook other side. Serve with butter and confectioners sugar, if desired.

Spiced Croutons

These spiced croutons make a great accompaniment for green salads, fruit, or chilled dessert soups. Package these croutons with a set of tongs for convenient serving.

- ½ French bread loaf (4 ounces), cubed
  Vegetable oil cooking spray
- ¼ teaspoon apple pie spice

Preheat oven to 375 degrees. Coat bread cubes evenly with cooking spray. Place in a resealable plastic bag; add spice. Seal bag, and shake to coat. Arrange bread cubes on a baking sheet.
Bake 10 to 15 minutes or until browned; cool on wire racks.
Yield: about 4 servings

Spicy Apple Butter Bread

Friends will savor the flavor and aroma of this cinnamon-scented bread. Package it alongside a jar of apple butter for slathering on bread slices.

- 1 tablespoon dry yeast
- 1 teaspoon brown sugar
- 1 cup warm water (100 degrees to 110 degrees)
- 1 tablespoon honey
- ½ cup apple butter
- 2½ cups bread flour
- 1 cup whole-wheat flour
- 1 teaspoon ground cinnamon
- ½ teaspoon salt
- ¼ cup toasted honey-flavored wheat germ
- 1 tablespoon milk

In a 2-cup liquid measuring cup, combine yeast, brown sugar, water, and honey; let stand 5 minutes. Stir in apple butter. In a large mixing bowl, combine yeast mixture, bread flour, and next 3 ingredients; beat at medium speed of an electric mixer until well blended.
Sprinkle wheat germ evenly over work surface. Turn dough out onto surface, and knead until smooth and elastic (about 10 minutes). Place in a well-greased bowl, turning to coat top. Cover and let rise in a warm place (85 degrees), free from drafts, 50 minutes or until doubled in size.
Punch dough down, and shape into an 8-inch round loaf. Place loaf on a greased baking sheet. Cover and let rise in a warm place, free from drafts, 30 minutes or until doubled in size. Brush loaf with milk. Preheat oven to 425 degrees. Bake 10 minutes. Reduce oven temperature to 375 degrees, and bake 10 minutes longer or until loaf sounds hollow when tapped. Remove loaf from baking sheet immediately; cool on a wire rack.
Yield: 1 loaf bread

Honey Whole-Wheat Bread

Start your gift giving with this wonderful bread wrapped in a holiday tea towel and tied with a bow and fresh greenery.

      4   cups whole-wheat flour, divided
     ½   cup nonfat milk powder
      1   tablespoon salt
      2   envelopes (¼ ounce each) dry yeast
      3   cups water, divided
     ½   cup honey
      2   tablespoons butter or margarine
      2   to 3 cups all-purpose flour

In a large bowl, beat 3 cups whole-wheat flour, milk powder, salt, and yeast at low speed of a heavy-duty electric mixer until combined.

Bring 2 cups water to a boil over medium heat; add honey and butter, stirring until butter melts. Remove from heat, and stir in 1 cup cold water. (Mixture will register about 120 degrees.)

Add honey mixture to flour mixture, beating at low speed 1 minute. Increase speed to medium, and beat 2 minutes. Gradually add remaining whole-wheat flour and enough all-purpose flour to make a soft dough.

Turn dough out onto a well floured surface, and knead until smooth and elastic (about 5 minutes). Place in a well-greased bowl, turning to coat top.

Cover and let rise in a warm place (85 degrees), free from drafts, 1 hour or until doubled in size.

Punch dough down, and divide into 2 equal portions. Roll each portion into a 10 x 15-inch rectangle. Roll each up jellyroll fashion, beginning with short edge. Fold ends under, and place each, seam side down, in a 5 x 9-inch loaf pan.

Cover and let rise in a warm place, free from drafts, 45 minutes or until doubled in size.

Preheat oven to 375 degrees. Bake 40 to 45 minutes, shielding with aluminum foil after 25 minutes to prevent excessive browning; cool on wire racks.

Yield: 2 loaves bread

Butternut-Oatmeal Bread

You'll love that this makes two loaves—eat one while it's hot, covered with butter, and give the other as a gift.

      2   envelopes (¼ ounce each) dry yeast
   1¼   cups warm water (100 degrees to
              110 degrees)
   5½   to 5¾ cups bread flour, divided
   1¼   cups mashed, cooked butternut squash
              (1 medium)
     ¼   cup molasses
     ¼   cup vegetable oil
      2   teaspoons salt
      1   cup quick-cooking oats, divided
      1   tablespoon water

In a 2-cup liquid measuring cup, combine yeast and 1¼ cups warm water; let stand 5 minutes. Combine yeast mixture, 3 cups flour, and next 4 ingredients in a large bowl; beat at medium speed of an electric mixer 2 minutes or until smooth. Set 2 tablespoons oats aside; gradually stir in remaining oats and 2 cups flour to make a moderately stiff dough.

Turn dough out onto a lightly floured surface. Knead until smooth and elastic (about 10 minutes), adding enough remaining flour, ¼ cup at a time, to prevent sticking. Place in a well-greased bowl, turning to coat top. Cover and let rise in a warm place (85 degrees), free from drafts, 35 minutes or until doubled in size.

Punch dough down; divide in half. Turn one portion out onto a lightly floured surface; knead 3 or 4 times. Roll into a 7 x 14-inch rectangle. Roll up, starting at short edge, pressing firmly to eliminate air pockets; pinch ends to seal. Place dough, seam side down, in a lightly greased 5 x 9-inch loaf pan sprinkled with 1½ teaspoons oats. Repeat procedure with remaining dough.

Brush loaves evenly with 1 tablespoon water; sprinkle evenly with remaining 1 tablespoon oats. Cover and let rise in a warm place, free from drafts, 25 minutes or until doubled in size.

Preheat oven to 350 degrees. Bake 35 minutes or until loaves sound hollow when tapped. Remove from pans immediately; cool on wire racks.

Yield: 2 loaves bread

Onion and Rosemary Bread

Onion and Rosemary Bread

Rosemary is the herb of remembrance. Combined with onion, it makes this savory bread a gift your recipient will never forget. Tie a sprig of rosemary alongside the gift tag to hint at the flavor.

> 1 envelope (¼ ounce) dry yeast
> 1 tablespoon sugar
> 1½ cups warm water (100 degrees to 110 degrees)
> 2 teaspoons salt
> ½ cup chopped onion
> 4 cups all-purpose flour
> 1 tablespoon olive oil
> 1½ tablespoons fresh rosemary
> ½ teaspoon coarse salt or ¼ teaspoon salt

In a large bowl, stir together yeast, sugar, and water, and let stand 5 minutes. Stir in 2 teaspoons salt, onion, and enough flour to form a soft dough. Turn dough out onto a floured surface, and knead until smooth and elastic (about 10 minutes). Place in a well-greased bowl, turning to coat top. Cover and let rise in a warm place (85 degrees), free from drafts, 45 minutes or until doubled in size.

Punch dough down. Shape into an 8-inch round on a greased baking sheet. Cover and let rise in a warm place, free from drafts, 30 minutes or until doubled in size. Carefully brush with oil; sprinkle with rosemary and ½ teaspoon coarse salt.

Preheat oven to 400 degrees. Bake 25 minutes or until golden; cool on a wire rack.

Yield: 1 loaf bread

Cheddar Cheese-Pepper Bread

Friends will enjoy this unique bread for holiday ham sandwiches, cheese toast, or just good snacking.

> 2½ cups all-purpose flour
> 2 teaspoons baking powder
> ¾ teaspoon baking soda
> ¾ teaspoon salt
> 1½ to 2½ teaspoons freshly ground black pepper
> 2 cups (8 ounces) shredded sharp Cheddar cheese
> 2 eggs
> 1 container (8 ounces) plain low-fat yogurt
> ½ cup butter, melted

Preheat oven to 375 degrees. In a large bowl, combine first 6 ingredients; make a well in center of mixture.

Stir together eggs, yogurt, and melted butter; add to flour mixture, stirring just until dry ingredients are moistened. Spoon into a greased and floured 4½ x 8½-inch loaf pan.

Bake 45 minutes or until a wooden pick inserted in center comes out clean. Cool in pan on a wire rack 10 minutes.

Yield: 1 loaf bread

Rhubarb Nut Bread *Big Batch*

Here's an out-of-the-ordinary fruit-nut bread to package for gift giving—your friends will be glad you did.

> 1 egg, lightly beaten
> 1½ cups firmly packed brown sugar
> 1 cup buttermilk
> ⅔ cup vegetable oil
> 1 teaspoon vanilla extract
> 2½ cups all-purpose flour
> 1 teaspoon baking soda
> 1 teaspoon salt
> 2 cups (¼-inch pieces) fresh or frozen rhubarb (about ½ pound)
> ½ cup chopped pecans
> ½ cup sugar
> ½ teaspoon ground cinnamon
> 1 tablespoon butter or margarine, softened

Preheat oven to 350 degrees. In a large bowl, combine egg, sugar, buttermilk, oil, and vanilla; stir well.

Combine flour, baking soda, and salt; add to brown sugar mixture, and stir just until blended. Fold in rhubarb and pecans. Pour batter into 2 well-greased 4½ x 8½-inch loaf pans.

Combine ½ cup sugar, cinnamon, and butter; stir with a fork until mixture is crumbly. Sprinkle mixture over batter.

Bake 1 hour or until a wooden pick inserted in center comes out clean. Cool in pans on wire racks 10 minutes; remove from pans, and cool completely on wire racks.

Yield: 2 loaves bread

Apple-Walnut Bread

Loaded with chopped apple and fresh orange juice and zest, this bread makes great use of holiday fruit baskets.

- ⅔ cup chopped walnuts
- 2½ cups all-purpose flour
- 1 cup sugar
- 2 teaspoons baking powder
- ½ teaspoon baking soda
- ¼ teaspoon salt
- 2½ teaspoons grated orange zest, divided
- 2 eggs
- ¾ cup fresh orange juice
- ½ cup walnut or vegetable oil
- 1½ cups peeled, chopped apple
- 2 tablespoons sugar

Preheat oven to 350 degrees. Bake walnuts in a shallow pan, stirring occasionally, 5 to 10 minutes or until toasted.

Stir together flour, 1 cup sugar, baking powder, baking soda, salt, and 2 teaspoons orange zest; make a well in center of mixture.

Stir together eggs, orange juice, and oil until blended. Stir into flour mixture just until moistened; fold in walnuts and apple. Spoon into a greased and floured 5 x 9-inch loaf pan.

Stir together remaining ½ teaspoon orange zest and 2 tablespoons sugar; sprinkle over batter.

Bake 55 minutes. Cover with aluminum foil, and bake 10 minutes longer or until a wooden pick inserted in center comes out clean. Cool in pan on a wire rack 10 minutes. Remove from pan, and cool completely on a wire rack.

Yield: 1 loaf bread

Orange Poppy Seed Bread

Orange juice distinguishes these pretty poppy seed loaves from the more familiar lemon-flavored variety. This recipe makes two loaves for gift giving—unless you eat one yourself!

- 3 eggs, beaten
- 2¼ cups sugar
- 1½ cups milk
- 1 cup vegetable oil
- 1½ teaspoons vanilla extract
- 1½ teaspoons butter flavoring
- 3 cups all-purpose flour
- 1½ teaspoons baking powder
- 1½ teaspoons salt
- 1½ teaspoons poppy seed
- ¾ cup sugar
- ¼ cup orange juice
- 1½ teaspoons butter flavoring
- ½ teaspoon vanilla extract

Preheat oven to 350 degrees. In a large bowl, combine eggs, sugar, milk, oil, 1½ teaspoons vanilla, and 1½ teaspoons butter flavoring. Combine flour, baking powder, salt, and poppy seed. Add flour mixture to egg mixture, stirring just until smooth. Pour batter into 2 greased 4½ x 8½-inch loaf pans.

Bake 1 hour or until a wooden pick inserted in center comes out clean. Cool in pans on wire racks 10 minutes; remove from pans.

Combine ¾ cup sugar and orange juice in a small saucepan. Cook over medium heat, stirring constantly, until sugar dissolves. Remove from heat, and stir in 1½ teaspoons butter flavoring and ½ teaspoon vanilla. Prick holes in each loaf with a wooden pick. Brush glaze over loaves while warm. Cool loaves completely on wire racks.

Yield: 2 loaves bread

Banana-Nut Bread

This bread bakes up nicely in disposable pans for gift giving. Double- or triple-batch it to fit your gift list.

- 1 cup sugar
- ½ cup vegetable shortening
- 2 eggs
- 3 small bananas, mashed
- 1 teaspoon vanilla extract
- 2 cups all-purpose flour
- 1 teaspoon baking powder
- ½ teaspoon baking soda
- 1 teaspoon salt
- ½ cup chopped walnuts, toasted

Preheat oven to 350 degrees. Beat sugar and shortening at medium speed of an electric mixer until creamy. Add eggs, banana, and vanilla, beating well.

Combine flour, baking powder, baking soda, and salt; add to banana mixture, beating until combined. Stir in chopped walnuts.

Pour into a greased and floured 4 x 8-inch loaf pan.

Bake 1 hour or until a wooden pick inserted in center comes out clean. Cool on a wire rack 10 minutes; remove loaf from pan, and cool completely on wire rack.

Yield: 1 loaf bread

Banana-Nut Bread

Apricot-Pecan Bread

Apricot-Pecan Bread [Big Batch]

Filled with chunks of apricot, this bread is great for Christmas giving. It's the perfect size to slide into a paper gift bag.

2½ cups dried apricots, chopped
 1 cup chopped pecans
 4 cups all-purpose flour, divided
 ¼ cup butter, softened
 2 cups sugar
 2 eggs
 4 teaspoons baking powder
 ½ teaspoon baking soda
 ½ teaspoon salt
 1½ cups orange juice

In a large bowl, combine chopped apricots and warm water to cover; let stand 30 minutes. Drain apricots. Stir in pecans and ½ cup flour; set aside.

Beat butter at medium speed of an electric mixer 2 minutes; gradually add sugar, beating well. Add eggs, 1 at a time, beating after each addition.

Combine remaining 3½ cups flour, baking powder, baking soda, and salt. Add to butter mixture alternately with orange juice, beginning and ending with flour mixture. Stir in apricot mixture.

Preheat oven to 350 degrees. Spoon into 2 greased and floured 4½ x 8½-inch loaf pans; let stand at room temperature 20 minutes.

Bake 1 hour or until a wooden pick inserted in center comes out clean. Cool in pans on a wire rack 10 to 15 minutes; remove from pans, and cool completely on wire rack.

Yield: 2 loaves bread

Honey-Oat Buns

The flavors of these buns are tried and true. Give them wrapped in a tea towel tucked inside a basket.

½ cup honey
 ⅓ cup vegetable oil
 1¾ cups water
 1⅔ to 2 cups bread flour, divided
 1 cup uncooked regular oats
 ½ cup unprocessed oat bran
 1½ teaspoons salt
 3 envelopes (¼ ounce each) dry yeast
 2 eggs
 2½ cups whole-wheat flour

In a saucepan, combine honey, oil, and water; heat to 120 degrees to 130 degrees.

Combine 1⅔ cups bread flour and next 4 ingredients in a large mixing bowl. Gradually add honey mixture and eggs, beating at low speed of a heavy-duty electric mixer until blended. Beat at medium speed 3 more minutes. Gradually stir in whole-wheat flour and enough remaining bread flour to form a soft dough.

Turn dough out onto a well floured surface. Knead until smooth and elastic (about 10 minutes). Place in a well-greased bowl, turning to grease top.

Cover and let rise in a warm place (85 degrees), free from drafts, 1 hour or until doubled in size.

Punch dough down; let rest 15 minutes. Divide into 12 portions; shape into buns. Place on greased baking sheets.

Cover and let rise 20 minutes or until doubled in size.

Preheat oven to 375 degrees. Bake 15 minutes or until golden.

Yield: 1 dozen buns

Bread Storage and Freezing

Bread tends to stale quickly, but proper storage can keep it fresher longer.

- Many people store their bread in the refrigerator in hopes of keeping it fresh. Bread actually will stale more quickly if stored in the refrigerator than if stored at room temperature. For optimal freshness, cover the bread in airtight plastic wrap and store at room temperature up to 5 days.

- If you plan on storing your bread for a longer period of time, store it in the freezer. Allow the bread to cool completely after baking, wrap it tightly in aluminum foil, and place it in a heavy-duty freezer bag. Bread stored this way can be frozen up to 3 months. When ready to serve, partially unwrap the bread and let it stand at room temperature until thawed. Reheat, uncovered, at 350 degrees until thoroughly heated, if desired.

Whole-Wheat Spirals

Whole-Wheat Spirals

These light wheat rolls will be a prize for whoever receives them—they received our highest test kitchen rating. Equal amounts of whole-wheat and regular flour keep them light and tender, while a final brush of melted butter after baking keeps them moist and glistening.

    2 envelopes (¼ ounce each) dry yeast
 1¾ cups warm water (100 degrees to
       110 degrees)
    ½ cup sugar
    2 teaspoons salt
    ½ cup butter or margarine, melted and
       divided
    1 egg, lightly beaten
 2¼ cups whole-wheat flour
 2¼ to 2½ cups all-purpose flour

In a 2-cup liquid measuring cup, combine yeast and warm water; let stand 5 minutes.

Combine yeast mixture, sugar, salt, ¼ cup melted butter, egg, and whole-wheat flour in a large mixing bowl; beat at medium speed of an electric mixer until well blended. Gradually stir in enough all-purpose flour to make a soft dough.

Turn dough out onto a well floured surface, and knead until smooth and elastic (about 5 minutes). Place in a well-greased bowl, turning to grease top.

Cover and let rise in a warm place (85 degrees), free from drafts, 30 minutes or until doubled in size.

Punch dough down, and divide in half; shape each portion into a 7 x 14-inch rectangle. Cut each rectangle into 14 (1 x 7-inch) strips. Roll each strip into a spiral, and place in well-greased muffin pans.

Cover and let rise in a warm place, free from drafts, 20 minutes or until doubled in size.

Preheat oven to 400 degrees. Bake 8 to 10 minutes or until golden. Remove from pans, and cool on wire racks. Brush with remaining ¼ cup melted butter.
Yield: about 2½ dozen rolls

Oatmeal Dinner Rolls

A classic for any holiday meal, these slightly sweet rolls make a great holiday gift.

    2 cups water
    1 cup quick-cooking oats
    3 tablespoons butter or margarine
    2 envelopes (¼ ounce each) dry yeast
    ½ cup warm water (100 degrees to
       110 degrees)
    1 tablespoon sugar
    4 cups all-purpose flour
 1½ teaspoons salt
    ⅓ cup firmly packed brown sugar

Bring 2 cups water to a boil in a medium saucepan; stir in oats and butter. Boil, stirring constantly, 1 minute. Remove from heat; cool to 110 degrees.

Stir together yeast, ½ cup warm water, and 1 tablespoon sugar in a 2-cup measuring cup, and let stand 5 minutes.

Beat oat mixture, yeast mixture, flour, salt, and brown sugar at medium speed of an electric mixer until smooth.

Turn dough out onto a lightly floured surface; knead until smooth and elastic (about 5 minutes). Place in a well-greased bowl, turning to coat top.

Cover and let rise in a warm place (85 degrees), free from drafts, 1 hour or until dough is doubled in size.

Punch dough down, and divide in half; shape each portion into 16 (1½-inch) balls. Place evenly into 2 lightly greased 9-inch round cake pans.

Cover and let rise in a warm place, free from drafts, 30 minutes or until doubled in size.

Preheat oven to 375 degrees. Bake 15 minutes or until golden brown.
Yield: 32 rolls

Butter Rolls

(pictured on page 30)

Deliver these rolls the day before Christmas so your friend will have homemade bread fresh for the feast.

> 2 envelopes (¼ ounce each) dry yeast
> ½ cup sugar, divided
> ½ cup warm water (100 degrees to 110 degrees)
> 4½ cups all-purpose flour
> 2 teaspoons salt
> ½ cup cold butter or margarine, cut into 8 pieces
> ½ cup cold milk
> 2 eggs, divided
> 1 tablespoon water
> 1 egg
> Sesame or poppy seed

In a 1-cup measuring cup, stir together yeast, 1 teaspoon sugar, and ½ cup water; let stand 5 minutes.

Process flour, remaining sugar, and salt in a food processor 10 seconds or until blended. Add butter; process 10 seconds or to consistency of coarse meal.

Add milk and 2 eggs to yeast mixture. With processor running, pour egg mixture through food chute. Process dough 20 seconds or until dry ingredients are moistened. Continue processing 1 minute. (Dough will be soft.) Place dough in a well-greased bowl, turning once to grease top. Cover and let rise in a warm place (85 degrees), free from drafts, 1 hour or until doubled in size. Punch dough down, and divide into fourths; shape each portion into 6 (1½-inch) balls. Place in a lightly greased 9 x 13-inch pan. Cover and let rise in a warm place (85 degrees), free from drafts, 40 minutes.

Preheat oven to 375 degrees. Beat together 1 tablespoon water and remaining egg; carefully brush over rolls, and sprinkle with sesame seed.

Bake 18 to 20 minutes or until golden brown.
Yield: 2 dozen rolls

Sour Cream Yeast Rolls

Cellophane and ribbon are all you need to make these rolls a showy gift. Make an advance offer to your holiday dinner host of a gift basket of these rolls ready to reheat.

> ½ cup sour cream
> ¼ cup butter or margarine
> ¼ cup sugar
> ½ teaspoon salt
> 1 envelope (¼ ounce) dry yeast
> ¼ cup warm water (100 degrees to 110 degrees)
> 1 egg, beaten
> 2 cups all-purpose flour
> Melted butter

In a saucepan over low heat, cook sour cream, butter, sugar, and salt, stirring occasionally, until butter melts. Cool to 100 degrees to 110 degrees.

Dissolve yeast in ¼ cup warm water in a large mixing bowl; let stand 5 minutes. Stir in sour cream mixture and egg. Gradually add flour to yeast mixture, mixing well. (Dough will be wet.) Cover and chill 8 hours.

Punch dough down. Shape into 36 (1-inch) balls; place 3 balls in each lightly greased muffin cup.

Cover and let rise in a warm place (85 degrees), free from drafts, 1 hour or until doubled in size.

Preheat oven to 375 degrees. Bake 10 to 12 minutes or until golden brown. Brush with melted butter. Freeze up to 1 month, if desired.
Yield: 1 dozen rolls

Directions for gift card: To reheat, wrap frozen rolls in aluminum foil, and bake at 400 degrees for 15 minutes or until thoroughly heated.

Proofing Dough

Proofing yeast dough (letting it rise) is an important step in developing good texture for yeast breads. Here's how we proof yeast dough in our test kitchens.

After kneading the dough, place it in a greased bowl, turning it to coat the top surface. Cover the bowl with a barely damp kitchen towel or lightly greased plastic wrap. The ideal proofing, or rising, temperature is 85 degrees. An oven with a pan of very hot water placed on the rack under the dough should provide this temperature, as well as a draft-free environment.

Rising is complete when the dough has doubled in size, unless the recipe specifies otherwise. To test the dough for doubled size, press two fingers ½ inch into the dough. If the indentation remains, the dough has risen enough and is ready to be shaped.

You can also make the dough ahead and let it rise in the refrigerator. It will take about 8 hours to rise at this cooler temperature, and it will keep there up to four days if the dough is made with water or three days if made with milk. Be sure to punch the dough down once each day.

Sour Cream Yeast Rolls

Cinnamon Breakfast Rolls

Cinnamon Breakfast Rolls

Bake these cinnamon rolls completely or give the chilled dough in a disposable baking pan along with baking directions. Either way, your friends will be all smiles.

    1 package (18.25 ounces) French vanilla
        cake mix
5¼ cups all-purpose flour
    2 envelopes (¼ ounce each) dry yeast
    1 teaspoon salt
2½ cups warm water (100 degrees to
        110 degrees)
    ½ cup sugar
    2 teaspoons ground cinnamon
    ½ cup butter or margarine, melted
    ½ cup raisins, divided
    ¾ cup chopped pecans, divided
    1 cup confectioners sugar
    3 tablespoons milk
    ½ teaspoon vanilla extract

In a large bowl, stir together cake mix, flour, yeast, salt, and water; cover and let rise in a warm place (85 degrees), free from drafts, 1 hour.

Combine ½ cup sugar and cinnamon.

Turn dough out onto a well floured surface; divide in half. Roll one portion into a 12 x 18-inch rectangle. Brush with half of butter; sprinkle with half of sugar mixture, half of raisins, and ¼ cup pecans.

Roll up starting at long edge; cut crosswise into 16 (1-inch-thick) slices. Place rolls in a lightly greased 9 x 13-inch pan. Repeat procedure with remaining rectangle. Cover and chill 8 hours.

Remove from refrigerator, and let stand 30 minutes.

Preheat oven to 350 degrees. Bake 20 to 25 minutes or until golden; cool slightly.

Stir together confectioners sugar, milk, and vanilla; drizzle over rolls. Sprinkle with remaining pecans.

Yield: 32 rolls

Cranberry Rolls

Package these sweet rolls in a single layer to protect the pretty glaze drizzled on top.

- 2 envelopes (¼ ounce each) rapid-rise yeast
- ¾ cup warm water (100 degrees to 110 degrees)
- 1 cup sugar, divided
- 3 cups all-purpose flour
- 6 tablespoons vegetable oil
- 2 eggs
- 1 teaspoon salt
- ½ cup butter or margarine, melted
- 1 teaspoon ground cinnamon
- 1 cup sweetened dried cranberries
- 12 large marshmallows
- 1 cup confectioners sugar
- 1 tablespoon milk
- ¼ teaspoon ground ginger

In a glass measuring cup, combine yeast and ¾ cup water; let stand 5 minutes.

Beat yeast mixture, ¼ cup sugar, and next 4 ingredients at low speed of an electric mixer until blended.

Turn dough out onto a well floured surface, and knead until smooth and elastic (about 4 minutes).

Cover and let rise in a warm place (85 degrees), free from drafts, 45 minutes or until doubled in size.

Punch dough down, and divide into 12 portions. Roll each portion into a 3-inch circle.

Brush circles lightly with butter, reserving remaining butter.

Combine remaining ¾ cup sugar and cinnamon; sprinkle evenly over circles. Place cranberries evenly in center of each circle, and top with a marshmallow.

Pull edges of circle to center, and pinch to seal; shape into a ball. Place, seam side down, in lightly greased muffin pans. Brush tops with reserved butter. Cover and chill 8 hours.

Remove from refrigerator, and let rise in a warm place, free from drafts, 30 minutes or until doubled in size.

Preheat oven to 400 degrees. Bake 12 minutes or until lightly browned; cool slightly.

Stir together confectioners sugar, milk, and ginger; drizzle over rolls.

Yield: 1 dozen rolls

Cream Cheese and Chocolate Danish

Get a head start on these gift loaves and freeze them to have on hand for quick gifts. Thaw them completely before frosting.

- ½ cup water
- ½ cup milk
- ¼ cup butter or margarine
- 4 to 5 cups all-purpose flour, divided
- ¾ cup sugar, divided
- 1 teaspoon salt
- 2 envelopes (¼ ounce each) dry yeast
- 2 eggs
- 1 package (8 ounces) cream cheese, softened
- 1 egg yolk
- Chocolate ready-to-spread frosting

In a small saucepan, combine water, milk, and butter; heat to 120 degrees to 130 degrees. (Butter does not need to melt.)

Combine ¼ cup flour, ½ cup sugar, salt, and yeast in a large mixing bowl. Gradually add warm milk mixture to flour mixture, beating 2 minutes at medium speed of an electric mixer. Add 2 eggs and ½ cup flour; beat at medium speed until mixture thickens. Beat 2 minutes; using a wooden spoon, gradually stir in enough remaining flour to make a soft dough.

Turn dough out onto a lightly floured surface, and knead until smooth and elastic (about 8 minutes). Place in a well-greased bowl, turning to coat top. Cover and let rise in a warm place (85 degrees), free from drafts, 1 hour or until doubled in size.

Beat cream cheese and remaining ¼ cup sugar at medium speed of mixer until fluffy. Add egg yolk, and beat well.

Punch dough down; turn out onto a lightly floured surface, and knead lightly 4 or 5 times. Divide dough into 4 equal portions. Roll one portion of dough into a 6 × 16-inch rectangle. Spread one-fourth of cream cheese mixture over dough, leaving a 1-inch border. Roll up dough, starting at short edge, pressing firmly to eliminate air pockets; pinch ends to seal. Place dough, seam side down, on a lightly greased baking sheet. Repeat procedure with 3 remaining portions.

Cut slits in top of each loaf at 1-inch intervals. Cover and let rise in a warm place, free from drafts, 50 minutes or until doubled in size.

Preheat oven to 350 degrees. Bake 18 to 20 minutes or until lightly browned. Cool completely on wire racks. Spread tops of loaves with chocolate ready-to-spread frosting.

Yield: 4 loaves bread

Cranberry Christmas Tree Bread

Cranberry Christmas Tree Bread

Not only does this tree-shaped loaf use a convenient frozen bread dough, it also uses purchased frosting. What a time-saving gift to make!

1½ cups fresh or frozen cranberries
¾ cup sugar
1 tablespoon fresh orange juice
1½ teaspoons grated orange zest
½ package (8 ounces) frozen bread dough, thawed
2 tablespoons butter, melted
⅓ cup chopped walnuts (optional)
¼ cup cream cheese-flavored ready-to-spread frosting

In a medium saucepan, combine cranberries, sugar, juice, and zest, stirring well. (Frozen berries do not have to thaw first.) Cook over medium-high heat, stirring constantly, until thickened (about 10 minutes). Set aside, and cool.

Roll dough into a 9 x 18-inch rectangle; brush with melted butter. Spread cranberry mixture over dough to within ½ inch of edges. Sprinkle with walnuts, if desired. Roll up dough, starting at long edge, pressing gently to contain filling; pinch ends to seal. Cut roll into 16 equal slices (about 1⅛ inch thick).

On lower third of a large greased baking sheet, arrange 5 slices, cut side up, in a row with edges touching. Form tree with additional rows of rolls, ending with 1 roll on top of tree and 1 roll on bottom for trunk.

Cover and let rise in a warm place (85 degrees), free from drafts, 30 to 45 minutes or until doubled in size.

Preheat oven to 350 degrees. Bake 20 minutes or until lightly browned. Carefully remove from baking sheet, and cool on a wire rack.

Place frosting in a 2-cup glass measuring cup. Microwave, uncovered, on high power (100%) for 20 to 25 seconds or until drizzling consistency; drizzle over bread.
Yield: 1 tree-shaped loaf

Easy Stollen

Commercial frozen bread dough is a real time saver but it can be fairly elastic and springy when you first start working with it. Don't be afraid to work the dough with the rolling pin and flatten it into shape.

½ cup raisins
½ cup chopped pecans
2 tablespoons chopped red candied cherries
2 tablespoons chopped green candied cherries
1½ teaspoons brandy or orange juice
1 loaf (16 ounces) frozen bread dough, thawed
1 tablespoon butter or margarine, melted
Sugar-Brandy Glaze

In a medium bowl, combine raisins, pecans, cherries, and juice; set aside.

Place bread dough on a lightly floured surface; flatten with a rolling pin to 1-inch thickness. Spoon fruit mixture in center of dough, and knead dough until fruit is evenly distributed.

Roll dough to an oval shape, ½ inch thick. Fold in half lengthwise; seal edges. Place dough on a well-greased baking sheet; brush with melted butter. Cover and let rise in a warm place (85 degrees), free from drafts, 40 minutes or until doubled in size.

Preheat oven to 350 degrees. Bake 25 to 30 minutes or until loaf sounds hollow when tapped. Cool 10 minutes on a wire rack; drizzle with Sugar-Brandy Glaze.
Yield: 1 loaf bread

Sugar-Brandy Glaze

1½ cups sifted confectioners sugar
1 tablespoon plus 2 teaspoons brandy or orange juice
1 tablespoon fresh lime juice

Combine confectioners sugar, brandy, and lime juice.
Yield: about ¾ cup glaze

Easy Vegetable Chowder, page 79;
Spinach Enchilada Casserole, page 64

Meals in Minutes

Sitting down to a nice meal can be the highlight of a family's day, and it's even more special when the cook doesn't have to do all the work. These ready-to-bake meals will be savored gifts.

Turkey Pot Pie with Biscuit Crust

Turkey Pot Pie with Biscuit Crust

This makes a welcome gift on a chilly winter day. Packaging is simple when you bake the pot pie in a disposable baking container and tie a bow around it for the finishing touch.

- ½ cup butter or margarine, divided
- 1 medium onion, diced and divided
- 2 medium carrots, chopped
- 2 ribs celery, chopped
- 1¼ teaspoons salt, divided
- ½ teaspoon pepper
- ⅓ cup dry white wine or chicken broth
- 2 cups chicken broth
- 1¼ cups all-purpose flour, divided
- ½ cup milk
- 1½ cups chopped cooked turkey
- ¾ cup frozen green peas, thawed
- 1 teaspoon baking powder
- ⅛ teaspoon baking soda
- ¼ cup fresh sage, minced
- ¼ cup shredded sharp Cheddar cheese
- ¼ cup buttermilk

In a Dutch oven, melt 2 tablespoons butter; add half of onion, carrot, and celery. Add 1 teaspoon salt and pepper; sauté 5 to 6 minutes or until tender. Add wine; cook 3 to 4 minutes or until reduced by half. Add broth; bring to a boil. Reduce heat, and simmer 15 minutes.

Stir together ½ cup flour and milk; add to wine mixture, and cook, stirring occasionally, 8 to 10 minutes or until thickened. Stir in turkey and peas. Pour into a 1½-quart disposable plastic baking container. Set aside.

Preheat oven to 425 degrees. Cut ¼ cup butter into pieces.

In a food processor, pulse butter pieces, remaining ¾ cup flour, remaining ¼ teaspoon salt, baking powder, and baking soda 4 to 6 times or until crumbly. Add remaining onion, sage, and cheese; with machine running, gradually add buttermilk through food chute, processing until dough forms a ball. Turn out onto a heavily floured surface; knead 3 or 4 times. Roll into a 10-inch circle. Place over turkey mixture, pressing to edges of dish to seal. Melt remaining 2 tablespoons butter; brush over dough. Make ¼-inch-deep slashes in top with a knife.

Bake pot pie, uncovered, 30 minutes or until golden brown.

Yield: about 4 servings

Cheesy Tortilla Casseroles

This recipe makes dinner to take to a couple of friends—or for a friend and you!

- 3 pounds lean ground beef
- 3 cans (10 ounces each) mild enchilada sauce
- 2 cans (10¾ ounces each) cream of mushroom soup, undiluted
- 15 corn tortillas (about 6-inch diameter), halved
- 2 cups (8 ounces) shredded Cheddar cheese, divided

Preheat oven to 350 degrees. In a Dutch oven, brown ground beef, stirring until it crumbles; drain. Stir in enchilada sauce and soup; spoon about 1 cup into the bottom of each of 2 lightly greased 7 x 11-inch baking dishes.

Layer 1 dish with one-fourth of tortillas, ¼ cup cheese, and one-fourth of remaining meat sauce. Repeat layers once. Repeat procedure in second dish.

Bake 30 minutes. Top with remaining 1 cup cheese; bake 5 more minutes.

Yield: 2 casseroles, 4 to 6 servings each

Chicken Enchilada Casseroles: Substitute 6 cups chopped cooked chicken for ground beef.

Hot Casseroles to Go

Our first three casseroles offer comfort food options that travel well hot from the oven when your gift is dinner to a friend. Select one of these recipes for neighbors or friends living within a short distance, and let them know dinner is on its way so no reheating is necessary. A green salad is all that's needed to round out these one-dish meals.

Blend of the Bayou

Celebrate the Bayou region with two of its most famous foods—fresh shrimp and lump crabmeat. Deliver this casserole hot from the oven with eager recipients awaiting dinner's arrival.

1⅓ pounds unpeeled medium-size fresh shrimp
2 tablespoons butter or margarine
1 large onion, chopped
1 green pepper, chopped
2 ribs celery, chopped
1 package (8 ounces) cream cheese, softened
½ cup butter or margarine, softened
1 pound fresh lump crabmeat
2 cups hot cooked rice
1 can (10¾ ounces) cream of mushroom soup, undiluted
1 jar (4½ ounces) whole mushrooms, drained
1 tablespoon garlic salt
1 teaspoon hot sauce
½ teaspoon ground red pepper
1 cup round buttery cracker crumbs (about 20 crackers)
1 cup (4 ounces) shredded sharp Cheddar cheese

Peel shrimp; devein if desired.

Preheat oven to 350 degrees. In a Dutch oven, melt 2 tablespoons butter over medium-high heat. Add onion, green pepper, and celery; sauté 10 minutes. Add shrimp; sauté 2 minutes. Remove from heat. Add cream cheese and ½ cup butter, stirring until cream cheese and butter melt. Stir in crabmeat and next 6 ingredients. Spoon mixture into a lightly greased 9 x 13-inch baking dish.

Stir together cracker crumbs and Cheddar cheese; sprinkle over shrimp mixture. Bake, uncovered, 25 to 30 minutes or until bubbly.

Yield: about 8 servings

You Make It; They Bake It

Here's an assortment of "take-and-bake" casseroles that can cover breakfast, lunch, or dinner. You assemble and chill them 4 to 6 hours, and then deliver them with baking instructions. Pack them in a cooler for delivery if your destination is more than a short drive away. They can chill up to 24 hours before baking. Of course, you can go ahead and bake them yourself with our directions for baking without chilling, if you prefer.

Chicken-and-Dressing Casserole

This clever casserole layers chicken, stuffing, and gravy into one. Deliver it assembled and chilled, along with directions for baking.

4 large chicken breast halves or 1 (2½ to 3 pound) broiler-fryer, cut up
1 can (10¾ ounces) cream of chicken soup, undiluted
1 can (10¾ ounces) cream of mushroom soup, undiluted
½ teaspoon poultry seasoning
1 package (8 ounces) herb-seasoned stuffing mix
½ cup butter or margarine, melted

Cook chicken in boiling water to cover 30 to 40 minutes or until tender. Remove chicken. Pour broth through a large wire-mesh strainer into a 4-cup liquid measuring cup, reserving 2½ cups broth. Skin, bone, and cut chicken into bite-size pieces; set aside.

Combine reserved broth, soups, and poultry seasoning; set aside.

Combine stuffing mix and butter; reserve ¼ cup stuffing mixture. Spoon half of remaining stuffing mixture into a lightly greased 9 x 13-inch disposable plastic baking container; top with half of chicken, and spoon half of soup mixture evenly over chicken. Repeat layers. Sprinkle with ¼ cup reserved stuffing mixture. Cover and chill unbaked casserole 4 to 6 hours and deliver with baking instructions. (To bake without chilling, preheat oven to 350 degrees and bake 30 to 40 minutes or until thoroughly heated.)

Yield: about 6 servings

Directions for gift card: Keep refrigerated until ready to bake, up to 24 hours. When ready to bake, remove casserole from refrigerator, and let stand at room temperature 20 minutes. Preheat oven to 350 degrees. Uncover casserole and bake 35 to 45 minutes or until thoroughly heated.

Adobe Chicken Casserole

This easy, cheesy casserole will please family members of all ages. It sports a mild Tex-Mex flavor but isn't too spicy.

  1 medium onion, chopped
  3 cloves garlic, minced
  2 tablespoons vegetable oil
  3 cups chopped cooked chicken
  2 cups cooked long-grain rice
  2 cups cooked brown rice
  1 can (14½ ounces) diced tomatoes, drained
  ½ teaspoon salt
  ½ teaspoon pepper
  1 carton (16 ounces) sour cream
  2 cans (4 ounces each) whole green chiles, drained and cut into strips
  3 cups (12 ounces) shredded Monterey Jack cheese
  1 can (2¼ ounces) sliced ripe olives, drained

In a medium skillet, cook onion and garlic in hot oil, stirring constantly, until tender. Combine onion mixture, chicken, and next 5 ingredients in a large bowl; stir well.

Spoon half of chicken mixture into a greased 3-quart disposable plastic baking container. Spoon half of sour cream over chicken mixture; top with half of chiles, half of cheese, and all of olives. Repeat layers, ending with cheese.

Cover and chill unbaked casserole 4 to 6 hours, and deliver with baking instructions. (To bake without chilling, preheat oven to 350 degrees, cover casserole, and bake 40 minutes. Uncover and bake 5 more minutes or until thoroughly heated. Let stand 10 minutes before serving.)
Yield: about 6 servings

Directions for gift card: Keep refrigerated until ready to bake, up to 24 hours. When ready to bake, remove casserole from refrigerator, and let stand at room temperature 20 minutes. Preheat oven to 350 degrees. Cover casserole and bake 45 minutes. Uncover and bake 15 more minutes or until thoroughly heated. Let stand 10 minutes before serving.

Chicken Noodle Casserole

All the pleasures of homestyle soup and more are wrapped up in this make-ahead casserole. Deliver it in a disposable baking dish along with a bag of preshredded Cheddar cheese to be added towards the end of baking.

  8 ounces uncooked spaghetti
  1 small onion, chopped
  1 small green pepper, chopped
  ¾ cup milk
  ½ teaspoon pepper
  ¼ teaspoon salt
  1 can (10¾ ounces) cream of chicken soup, undiluted
  2 cups chopped cooked chicken breast
  1 jar (4½ ounces) sliced mushrooms, drained
  1 jar (4 ounces) diced pimiento, drained
  1 cup (4 ounces) shredded sharp Cheddar cheese

Cook spaghetti according to package directions. Drain.

Meanwhile, coat a Dutch oven with cooking spray; place over medium heat until hot. Add onion and green pepper; sauté 5 minutes or until tender.

Combine onion mixture, milk, pepper, salt, and soup; stir well. Combine pasta, chicken, mushrooms, and pimiento; toss gently. Pour soup mixture over pasta mixture; toss until pasta is well coated.

Spoon mixture into a lightly greased 7 x 11-inch disposable plastic baking container. Cover and chill unbaked casserole 4 to 6 hours, and deliver with baking instructions. (To bake without chilling, preheat oven to 375 degrees and bake, uncovered, 25 minutes. Sprinkle with cheese and bake, uncovered, 5 more minutes or until cheese melts.)
Yield: about 6 servings

Directions for gift card: Keep refrigerated until ready to bake, up to 24 hours. When ready to bake, remove casserole from refrigerator and let stand at room temperature 20 minutes. Preheat oven to 375 degrees. Bake, uncovered, 30 minutes. Sprinkle with 1 cup Cheddar cheese; bake, uncovered, 5 more minutes or until cheese melts.

Spinach Enchilada Casserole

(pictured on page 58)

This make-ahead, take-along, one-dish-meal casserole is made with a base of ground beef and butter-dipped corn tortillas, then packed to the brim with a spicy mix of chiles and cheese. No need for the recipient even to add bread with the generous layering of tortillas.

1 package (10 ounces) frozen chopped spinach, thawed
2 pounds ground chuck
1 medium onion, chopped
1 can (10 ounces) diced tomatoes and green chiles, undrained
½ teaspoon salt
½ teaspoon ground cumin
¼ teaspoon garlic powder
¼ teaspoon pepper
1 can (10¾ ounces) cream of mushroom soup, undiluted
1 can (10¾ ounces) golden mushroom soup, undiluted
1 container (8 ounces) sour cream
⅓ cup milk
12 corn tortillas (about 6-inch diameter)
¼ cup butter or margarine, melted
1 can (4.5 ounces) chopped green chiles, undrained
2 cups (8 ounces) shredded sharp Cheddar cheese, divided

Drain spinach in a colander, pressing with paper towels to remove excess moisture; set aside.

Cook ground chuck and onion in a large skillet, stirring until beef crumbles and is no longer pink; drain and return to skillet. Stir in reserved spinach, diced tomatoes and green chiles, and next 4 ingredients; set aside.

Stir together soups, sour cream, and milk; set aside.

Dip tortillas in melted butter. Layer half of tortillas in a greased 9 x 13-inch disposable plastic baking container. Top with meat mixture; sprinkle with chopped green chiles. Sprinkle 1½ cups cheese over green chiles. Top with remaining half of tortillas dipped in butter; spread soup mixture over tortillas. Sprinkle with remaining ½ cup cheese; cover and chill unbaked casserole 4 to 6 hours, and deliver with baking instructions. (To bake without chilling, preheat oven to 350 degrees. Bake, uncovered, 40 minutes or until bubbly. Let stand 10 minutes before serving.)
Yield: 8 to 10 servings

Directions for gift card: Keep refrigerated until ready to bake, up to 24 hours. When ready to bake, remove casserole from refrigerator, and let stand at room temperature 20 minutes. Preheat oven to 350 degrees. Bake, uncovered, 45 minutes or until bubbly. Let stand 10 minutes before serving.

Shrimp-and-Chicken Casserole

Make this a double gift when you place the casserole in a glass dish inside a handsome casserole holder.

4 cups water
1 pound unpeeled medium-size fresh shrimp*
2 packages (16 ounces each) frozen broccoli flowerets, thawed and well drained
1 can (10¾ ounces) cream of chicken soup, undiluted
1 can (10¾ ounces) cream of celery soup, undiluted
1 cup mayonnaise
3 tablespoons lemon juice
¼ teaspoon ground white pepper
4 cups chopped cooked chicken
1 cup (4 ounces) shredded Cheddar cheese
¼ teaspoon paprika

Bring 4 cups water to a boil; add shrimp, and cook 3 to 5 minutes or just until shrimp turn pink. Drain and rinse with cold water. Peel shrimp, and devein, if desired. Set aside.

Spread broccoli evenly in a lightly greased 9 x 13-inch baking dish.

Stir together cream of chicken soup and next 4 ingredients until blended. Spread about one-third mixture evenly over broccoli; top with chicken and shrimp. Spread remaining soup mixture evenly over chicken and shrimp. Sprinkle with Cheddar cheese and paprika. Cover and chill unbaked casserole 4 to 6 hours, and deliver with baking instructions. (To bake without chilling, preheat oven to 350 degrees. Cover and bake 25 minutes. Uncover and bake 10 more minutes or until hot and bubbly.)
Yield: about 10 servings

*Substitute 1 package (16 ounces) frozen ready-to-eat cooked shrimp, if desired. Thaw according to package directions, and remove tails, if necessary. Omit cooking shrimp.

Note: 1 (1½ pound) whole roasted chicken yields 4 cups chopped cooked chicken.

Directions for gift card: Keep refrigerated until ready to bake, up to 24 hours. When ready to bake, remove casserole from refrigerator and let stand at room temperature 20 minutes. Preheat oven to 350 degrees. Bake, covered, 30 minutes. Uncover, and bake 15 more minutes or until hot and bubbly.

Shrimp-and-Chicken Casserole

Creamy Ham Casseroles

This duo of 8-inch casseroles makes great gifts for smaller families or newlyweds.

8 ounces uncooked egg noodles
1 can (10¾ ounces) cream of mushroom soup, undiluted
1 container (8 ounces) chive-and-onion-flavored cream cheese, softened
⅔ cup milk
2 cups chopped ham
3 cups fresh broccoli flowerets
6 baby carrots, chopped
1 package (8 ounces) shredded mozzarella cheese
1 cup (4 ounces) shredded Cheddar cheese
½ cup crushed seasoned croutons

Cook pasta according to package directions; drain.

Stir together soup, cream cheese, and milk in a large bowl. Stir in pasta, ham, broccoli, and carrots. Spoon half of ham mixture into 2 lightly greased 8-inch square disposable plastic baking containers.

Combine cheeses. Sprinkle half of cheese mixture over casseroles. Spoon remaining ham mixture over cheeses.

Combine remaining cheese mixture with croutons. Sprinkle over casseroles. Cover unbaked casseroles with lids, freeze up to 1 month, and deliver with baking instructions. (To bake without freezing, preheat oven to 400 degrees. Bake, uncovered, 30 minutes or until lightly browned.)

Yield: 2 casseroles, 3 to 4 servings each

Directions for gift card: Thaw frozen casserole in refrigerator overnight. Preheat oven to 400 degrees. Bake, covered, 30 minutes. Uncover, and bake 5 more minutes or until lightly browned.

Creamy Ham Casserole

Artichoke and Smoked Ham Strata

Trendy ingredients distinguish this casserole for the gourmets on your gift list. Sourdough bread imparts its distinctive tanginess to this savory bread pudding layered with smoked ham, marinated artichoke hearts, and three cheeses. Note that a one-pound loaf of sourdough bread with crust removed will give you just the right amount of bread cubes.

- 2 cups milk
- ¼ cup olive oil
- 8 cups (1-inch) cubed sourdough bread
- 1½ cups whipping cream
- 5 eggs
- 3 cloves garlic, minced
- 1½ teaspoons salt
- ¾ teaspoon ground white pepper
- ½ teaspoon ground nutmeg
- 3 packages (4 ounces each) goat cheese, crumbled
- 2 tablespoons chopped fresh sage
- 1 tablespoon chopped fresh thyme leaves
- 1½ teaspoons herbes de Provence
- ¾ pound smoked ham, chopped
- 3 jars (6½ ounces each) marinated artichoke hearts, drained
- 1 cup (4 ounces) shredded fontina cheese
- 1½ cups grated Parmesan cheese

In a large bowl, combine milk and oil; add bread cubes. Let stand 10 minutes.

Whisk together whipping cream and next 5 ingredients in a large bowl. Stir in goat cheese.

Combine sage, thyme, and herbes de Provence in a small bowl.

Place half of bread mixture in a lightly greased 9 x 13-inch disposable plastic baking container. Top with half each of ham, artichoke hearts, herb mixture, and cheeses. Pour half of cream mixture over cheeses. Repeat layers, ending with cream mixture. Cover unbaked casserole and chill 4 to 6 hours, and deliver with baking instructions.
Yield: about 8 servings

Directions for gift card: Keep refrigerated until ready to bake, up to 24 hours. When ready to bake, remove casserole from refrigerator, and let stand at room temperature 20 minutes. Preheat oven to 350 degrees. Bake, uncovered, 55 minutes or until set and lightly browned.

Ham and Cornbread Casserole

For a full-meal gift, package this quick casserole with a pre-packaged salad kit.

- 2 cups frozen mixed vegetables, slightly thawed
- 1½ cups cubed cooked ham
- 1 package (8 ounces) dry cornbread stuffing mix
- 2 cups milk
- 3 eggs, beaten
- ¼ teaspoon salt
- ¼ teaspoon freshly ground pepper
- 1 cup (4 ounces) shredded sharp Cheddar cheese

In a large bowl, combine vegetables, ham, and stuffing mix; pour mixture into a greased 7 x 11-inch disposable plastic baking container.

Combine milk, eggs, salt, and pepper in a bowl, stirring well; pour over cornbread mixture. Sprinkle with cheese.

Cover unbaked casserole and chill 4 to 6 hours, and deliver with baking instructions.
Yield: about 6 servings

Directions for gift card: Keep refrigerated until ready to bake, up to 24 hours. When ready to bake, remove casserole from refrigerator, and let stand at room temperature 20 minutes. Preheat oven to 350 degrees. Cover and bake 35 minutes. Uncover, and bake 5 to 10 more minutes or until golden.

Disposable Containers You Can't Live Without

Several disposable containers are now manufactured to assist the busy cook in the storage and transportation of baked goods. Of course, you can always give a casserole or strata in a glass dish, making the glass dish a part of the gift. But if you're looking for a less expensive route, purchase a set of disposable plastic or aluminum baking containers from your supermarket. You will find that they are inexpensive, convenient, and made for baking in the oven. And they make ideal gift containers—perfect for when the holidays roll around.

Vegetable-Cheese Strata

Vegetable-Cheese Strata

Sweet red and green peppers make this strata burst with color. Cushion the dish in a basket with a decorative dish towel.

    ¾ cup diced onion
    ½ cup diced green onions
    I package (8 ounces) sliced fresh mushrooms
    2 tablespoons olive oil
    I sweet red pepper, cut into thin strips
    I green pepper, cut into thin strips
    5 cups (1-inch) cubed Italian bread (about
         I loaf)
  1½ cups (6 ounces) shredded Cheddar cheese
    ½ cup shredded Parmesan cheese
    6 eggs
  1¾ cups milk
    I tablespoon Dijon mustard
    ½ teaspoon salt
    ½ teaspoon pepper
    ¼ teaspoon hot sauce

In a skillet, sauté onions and mushrooms in hot oil until tender; stir in sweet peppers. Cook, stirring often, 10 minutes or until liquid evaporates.

Spread 2½ cups bread cubes in a lightly greased 7 x 11-inch baking dish. Top with half of vegetable mixture, and sprinkle with ¾ cup Cheddar cheese and ¼ cup Parmesan cheese. Repeat procedure with remaining bread cubes, vegetable mixture, and cheeses.

Whisk together eggs and remaining ingredients; pour over strata. Cover unbaked strata and chill 4 to 6 hours, and deliver with baking instructions.
Yield: about 6 servings

Directions for gift card: Keep refrigerated until ready to bake, up to 24 hours. When ready to bake, remove strata from refrigerator, and let stand at room temperature 20 minutes. Preheat oven to 350 degrees. Bake, uncovered, 45 minutes or until set.

Sweet Onion-Gruyère Strata

We love the flavor and layered look of this strata, with paper-thin prosciutto providing a slight but welcome salty sensation. It's a perfect make-ahead gift for brunch.

    4 cups chopped Vidalia or other sweet onion
    2 tablespoons olive oil
  2½ cups milk
    ½ teaspoon salt
    ¼ teaspoon dry mustard
    ⅛ teaspoon ground black pepper
    4 eggs, beaten
    I cup (4 ounces) chopped ham
    8 cups (½-inch) cubed French bread (about
         I loaf)
    I cup (4 ounces) shredded Gruyère, Jarlsberg,
         or Swiss cheese

In a large nonstick skillet, cook onion in hot oil over medium heat until onion begins to caramelize.

Combine milk, salt, mustard, pepper, and egg in a large bowl, and stir with a whisk until mixture is well blended. Stir in onion and ham. Add bread, tossing gently to coat.

Arrange half of bread mixture in a single layer in an 7 x 11-inch disposable plastic baking container. Sprinkle with ½ cup cheese; top with remaining bread mixture, and remaining cheese. Cover unbaked strata and chill 4 to 6 hours, and deliver with baking instructions.
Yield: about 8 servings

Directions for gift card: Keep refrigerated until ready to bake, up to 24 hours. When ready to bake, remove strata from refrigerator, and let stand at room temperature 20 minutes. Preheat oven to 350 degrees. Bake, uncovered, 40 minutes or until set.

Christmas Morning Brunch Casserole

Make no mistake. This is a hearty dish—bubbling full of bacon, eggs, and sharp Cheddar cheese. What a grand gift to deliver Christmas Eve for an easy and special morning meal.

  2 large baking potatoes, unpeeled and cubed
  1/4 cup butter or margarine
  1/4 cup all-purpose flour
  1 cup milk
  1 cup half and half
  4 cups (16 ounces) shredded sharp Cheddar cheese
  1 teaspoon dried Italian seasoning
  1/2 teaspoon pepper
  12 hard-cooked eggs, sliced
  1 pound bacon, cooked and coarsely crumbled
  2 cups soft whole-wheat breadcrumbs (4 slices bread)
  3 tablespoons butter or margarine, melted

Cook potatoes in boiling water to cover in a large saucepan 15 minutes or until just tender. Drain and cool potatoes.

Melt 1/4 cup butter in a heavy saucepan over medium-low heat; add flour, stirring until smooth. Cook, stirring constantly, 1 minute. Gradually add milk and half and half; cook over medium heat, stirring constantly, until thickened and bubbly. Add cheese, Italian seasoning, and pepper, stirring constantly until cheese melts. Remove from heat.

Layer half each of egg slices, bacon, and cheese sauce in a lightly greased 9 x 13-inch disposable plastic baking container. Top with potatoes. Top with remaining egg slices, bacon, and cheese sauce.

Combine breadcrumbs and 3 tablespoons melted butter; sprinkle over casserole. Cover and chill 4 to 6 hours, and deliver with baking instructions. (To bake without chilling, preheat oven to 350 degrees and bake, uncovered, 30 minutes or until thoroughly heated.)

Yield: about 10 servings

Directions for gift card: Keep refrigerated until ready to bake, up to 24 hours. When ready to bake, remove casserole from refrigerator, and let stand at room temperature 30 minutes. Bake, uncovered, 30 minutes or until thoroughly heated.

Chilaquiles Casserole

Nestled in a basket, this casserole is popping with flavor. Garnish this gift with jalapeño slices to give a hint of its southwestern flair.

  8 eggs, beaten
  1 can (8 1/2 ounces) cream-style corn
  1 can (4.5 ounces) chopped green chiles, undrained
  2 cups cottage cheese
  1 cup milk
  3/4 teaspoon salt
  1/2 teaspoon black pepper
  1/8 teaspoon ground red pepper
  6 corn tortillas (about 6-inch diameter), cut into 1/2-inch strips
  1 package (8 ounces) shredded Cheddar and mozzarella cheese blend

In a large bowl, combine first 8 ingredients; stir in tortilla strips and cheese. Pour mixture into a lightly greased 9 x 13-inch disposable aluminum baking container.

Cover unbaked casserole and chill 4 to 6 hours, and deliver with baking instructions. (To bake without chilling, preheat oven to 350 degrees. Bake, uncovered, 45 minutes or until set.)

Yield: about 8 servings

Directions for gift card: Keep refrigerated until ready to bake, up to 24 hours. When ready to bake, remove casserole from refrigerator, and let stand at room temperature 20 minutes. Preheat oven to 350 degrees. Bake, uncovered, 45 minutes or until set. Let stand 15 minutes before serving. Garnish with jalapeño slices and cilantro. Cut into squares, and serve with salsa.

Chilaquiles Casserole

French Toast Soufflé

French Toast Soufflé

Bake this soufflé in a blue and white speckled disposable aluminum baking container—it will complement the confectioners sugar sprinkled on top. A firm white bread produces the best texture in this make-ahead breakfast casserole.

- 10 cups (1-inch) cubed sturdy white bread
- 1 package (8 ounces) cream cheese, softened
- 8 eggs
- 1½ cups milk
- ⅔ cup half and half
- ½ cup maple syrup
- ½ teaspoon vanilla extract

Place bread cubes in a greased 9 x 13-inch disposable aluminum baking container. Beat cream cheese at medium speed of an electric mixer until smooth. Add eggs, 1 at a time, mixing well after each addition. Add milk, half and half, ½ cup maple syrup, and vanilla, and mix until smooth. Pour cream cheese mixture over top of bread; cover unbaked soufflé and refrigerate 4 to 6 hours, and deliver with baking instructions.
Yield: about 12 servings

Directions for gift card: Keep refrigerated until ready to bake, up to 24 hours. When ready to bake, remove soufflé from refrigerator, and let stand at room temperature 20 minutes. Preheat oven to 375 degrees. Bake, uncovered, 50 minutes or until set. Sprinkle soufflé with confectioners sugar, and serve with maple syrup.

Southwestern Breakfast Casserole

You can assemble this entire breakfast casserole gift up to a month ahead. Bake the corn muffin mix ahead; store in an airtight container in the freezer for a couple of days. Assemble the casserole according to directions; cover and freeze up to a month. Deliver it frozen with thawing and baking directions on the gift card.

- 1 package (8½ ounces) corn muffin mix
- 3 cups (½-inch) cubed French bread
- 8 ounces hot breakfast Italian sausage
- 1 cup chopped onion
- 2½ cups milk
- 1 teaspoon ground cumin
- ⅛ teaspoon black pepper
- 1 can (10 ounces) diced tomatoes and green chiles, undrained
- 4 eggs, beaten
- 1 cup (4 ounces) shredded Monterey Jack or mild Cheddar cheese, divided

Prepare corn muffin mix according to package directions; cool. Crumble muffins into a large bowl; stir in bread. Set aside.

Remove casings from sausage. Cook sausage and onion in a large nonstick skillet over medium heat until browned, stirring to crumble. Drain.

Combine milk, cumin, pepper, tomatoes and green chiles, and eggs; stir with a whisk until well blended. Add sausage mixture; stir well. Stir into bread mixture. Spoon half of bread mixture into a lightly greased 9 x 13-inch disposable plastic baking container. Top with ½ cup cheese. Spoon remaining bread mixture over cheese, and sprinkle with remaining cheese. Cover unbaked casserole and refrigerate 4 to 6 hours or freeze up to 1 month. Deliver with baking instructions.
Yield: about 8 servings

Directions for gift card: Thaw frozen casserole in refrigerator (about 24 hours). Let stand at room temperature 20 minutes. Preheat oven to 350 degrees. Bake casserole, uncovered, 1 hour or until set. Let stand 10 minutes before serving.

Walnut-Rice Dressing

This raisin-nut rice dressing makes a nice accompaniment for roast chicken, turkey, or pork. You can bake it immediately or spoon it into a disposable baking dish and deliver as a gift along with reheating instructions.

2¼ cups chicken broth
  1 cup uncooked long-grain rice
  1 tablespoon butter or margarine
  ¾ cup chopped onion
  ¾ cup chopped celery
  ½ cup raisins
  ½ cup chopped walnuts, toasted
  3 tablespoons honey
  ¼ teaspoon salt
  ¼ teaspoon pepper
  ¼ teaspoon ground allspice
  1 teaspoon grated lemon zest
  1 tablespoon lemon juice

In a medium saucepan, bring chicken broth to a boil; add rice. Reduce heat, and cook 20 minutes or until rice is tender. Remove from heat, and set aside.

Melt butter in a large skillet; add onion and celery, and cook over medium heat, stirring constantly, until crisp-tender. Add rice, raisins, walnuts, and remaining ingredients; toss gently. Serve immediately or spoon into a 2-quart disposable plastic baking container. Cover and chill 4 to 6 hours, and deliver along with reheating instructions.
Yield: about 6 servings

Directions for gift card: Keep refrigerated until ready to serve, up to 24 hours. When ready to serve, remove dressing from refrigerator, and let stand at room temperature 20 minutes. Preheat oven to 375 degrees. Reheat, uncovered, 20 minutes or until thoroughly heated.

Asparagus and Leek Strata

Buttered and golden herbed breadcrumbs make a pretty topping for this brunch or supper bread pudding. Package the breadcrumb mixture separately and deliver along with the casserole and baking directions.

  1 tablespoon butter or margarine
1½ pounds fresh asparagus spears, cut into
      1-inch slices
  3 small leeks, thinly sliced
  ½ cup water
  1 tablespoon chopped fresh parsley, divided
  1 tablespoon fresh tarragon leaves
      (or 1 teaspoon dried), divided
1½ teaspoons grated lemon zest
  ¾ teaspoon salt, divided
  ½ teaspoon black pepper, divided
  6 slices (1 ounce each) firm white sandwich
      bread
  1 cup (4 ounces) shredded fontina cheese, divided
  ½ cup freshly grated Parmesan cheese
2½ cups milk
  4 eggs
1½ cups freshly prepared breadcrumbs (about
      3 slices bread)

In a large nonstick skillet, melt butter over medium-high heat; add asparagus, leeks, and water. Bring to a boil; cover, reduce heat, and simmer 10 minutes or until tender, stirring occasionally. Drain; stir in 2 teaspoons parsley, 1½ teaspoons tarragon, lemon zest, ½ teaspoon salt, and ¼ teaspoon pepper.

Arrange half of bread slices in a single layer in a lightly greased 9 x 13-inch disposable plastic baking container. Top bread slices with half of asparagus mixture, and sprinkle with ½ cup fontina cheese. Repeat procedure with remaining bread, asparagus mixture, and ½ cup each fontina and Parmesan cheese.

Combine remaining ¼ teaspoon salt, remaining ¼ teaspoon pepper, milk, and eggs, and stir with a whisk until blended. Pour milk mixture over strata. Cover unbaked strata, and chill 4 to 6 hours.

Combine breadcrumbs, remaining 1 teaspoon parsley, and 1½ teaspoons tarragon. Package in a resealable plastic bag and deliver along with chilled casserole and baking instructions.
Yield: about 6 servings

Directions for gift card: Keep refrigerated until ready to bake, up to 24 hours. When ready to bake, remove strata from refrigerator, and let stand at room temperature 20 minutes. Sprinkle with breadcrumb mixture and dot with butter or spray with cooking spray. Bake, uncovered, 40 minutes or until set. Garnish with fresh tarragon leaves, if desired.

Asparagus and Leek Strata

Bean-and-Pasta Soup Mix

Bean-and-Pasta Soup Mix

The recipient of this gift will be thrilled to put this effortless meal together—they only have to add onion and garlic to the mix! This version makes one gift, but it's easy to set up an assembly line to make many more.

- 1 cup dried navy beans
- 1 cup dried black beans
- ½ cup uncooked small shell pasta
- ¼ cup dried tomato bits
- 1 bay leaf
- 3 tablespoons chicken bouillon granules
- 1 tablespoon dried parsley flakes
- 1 teaspoon dried basil leaves
- 1 teaspoon dried oregano leaves
- 1 teaspoon pepper
- ½ teaspoon dried rosemary leaves

Place beans in a small heavy-duty resealable plastic bag; tie or seal bag.

Combine pasta and remaining ingredients in a small heavy-duty resealable plastic bag; tie or seal bag.

Yield: enough for 1 recipe

Directions for gift card: Sort and wash beans. Place in a large Dutch oven. Cover with water 2 inches above beans. Soak 8 hours; drain. Sauté 1 large onion, chopped, and 2 cloves garlic, minced, in 2 tablespoons hot olive oil in Dutch oven. Add 3 quarts water and beans. Bring to a boil; cover, reduce heat, and simmer 1½ hours. Stir in pasta mixture. Bring to a boil; reduce heat, and simmer, uncovered, 30 minutes.

Yield: about 10 cups soup

Spicy Jambalaya Mix

Here's an easy recipe to make lots of gifts. It yields enough for four gifts, and it doubles or triples easily to make even more.

- 4 cups uncooked long-grain rice
- ¼ cup dried onion flakes
- ¼ cup dried green pepper flakes
- ¼ cup dried parsley flakes
- 3 tablespoons beef bouillon granules
- 2 teaspoons dried shredded green onions
- 2 teaspoons black pepper
- 1 teaspoon garlic powder
- 1 teaspoon dried thyme leaves
- 1 teaspoon ground red pepper

Combine all ingredients. Divide mixture equally into fourths (about 1¼ cups each) and package in 4 heavy-duty resealable plastic bags. Store in an airtight container in a cool, dry place.

Yield: about 5 cups mix (4 gifts)

Directions for gift card: Combine rice mix, 2 cups water, and 1 (8-ounce) can tomato sauce in a Dutch oven. Bring to a boil; cover, reduce heat, and simmer 20 minutes. Stir in 1 pound smoked sausage (cut into ¼-inch slices) and 1 cup chopped cooked ham or chicken. Cook until thoroughly heated.

Yield: about 6 servings

Turkey and Navy Bean Chili

Turkey and Navy Bean Chili

The smoky essence of Southwest cuisine infuses this soup. Charred chiles, tomatillos, and roasted garlic are theme flavors that will satisfy even the most gourmet friends on your gift list. Package Chili-Cheese Croutons separately for recipients to serve on top.

    1 package (16 ounces) dried navy beans
    4 fresh poblano chile peppers
    4 tomatillos, husks removed
    1 large head garlic
    2 tablespoons olive oil, divided
    1 medium onion, chopped
    1 carton (32 ounces) chicken broth
    1 can (14½ ounces) chicken broth
    5 cups chopped cooked turkey
    1 tablespoon ground cumin
    ½ teaspoon salt
    ¼ teaspoon freshly ground pepper
       Chili-Cheese Croutons

Place beans in a large Dutch oven; add water 2 inches above beans. Bring to a boil. Boil 2 minutes; cover, remove from heat, and let stand 1 hour. Drain; return beans to pan.

Cut peppers in half lengthwise; discard seeds and membranes. Place peppers, skin sides up, on an aluminum foil-lined baking sheet, and flatten with palm of hand. Add whole tomatillos to baking sheet. Broil 5½ inches from heat 15 to 20 minutes or until blistered and charred, turning tomatillos once.

Place peppers in a heavy-duty resealable plastic bag; seal and let stand 10 minutes to loosen skins. Peel peppers; coarsely chop peppers and tomatillos.

Reduce oven temperature to 425 degrees. Cut off pointed end of garlic; place garlic on a piece of aluminum foil, and drizzle with 1 tablespoon oil. Fold foil to seal. Bake 30 minutes; cool. Squeeze pulp from garlic cloves; set aside.

Sauté onion in remaining 1 tablespoon hot oil until tender; add to beans. Add peppers, tomatillos, chicken broth, and next 4 ingredients. Bring to a boil; cover, reduce heat, and simmer 1 hour and 45 minutes or just until beans are tender. Stir in roasted garlic. Simmer 10 more minutes.

Cool chili; package in 3 quart-size jars for gift giving. Chill up to 24 hours, and deliver with reheating instructions. Prepare and package croutons separately to accompany soup.
Yield: about 3 quarts chili

Directions for gift card: Keep refrigerated until ready to serve, up to 24 hours. When ready to serve, cook chili over low heat just until reheated. Garnish with chopped fresh cilantro and sour cream, if desired, and serve with croutons on top.

Chili-Cheese Croutons

    16 French baguette slices (½ inch thick each)
    ½ cup (2 ounces) finely shredded Monterey Jack
        cheese
    ⅓ cup butter or margarine, softened
    2½ teaspoons chili powder

Preheat oven to 375 degrees. Place baguette slices on a baking sheet. Bake 5 minutes, turning slices once.

Stir together cheese, softened butter, and chili powder. Spread cheese mixture onto croutons. Bake 7 more minutes.
Yield: about 8 servings

Easy Vegetable Chowder

(pictured on page 58)

This recipe makes 3 quarts of cheesy vegetable chowder. Package it in quart-size canning jars for gift giving.

    22 new potatoes (about 10 pounds)
    4 large carrots
    2 large onions
    6 tablespoons olive oil
    4 cans (10¾ ounces each) Cheddar cheese
        soup, undiluted
    8 cups water
    2 envelopes (1.15 ounces each) dry onion
        soup mix
    2 teaspoons pepper
    1 cup sliced green onions

Cut potatoes into ½-inch cubes and carrots into ½-inch slices; coarsely chop onion.

Sauté vegetables in hot oil in a Dutch oven until tender.

Stir together Cheddar cheese soup, water, soup mix, and pepper until blended; add to vegetable mixture. Bring to a boil; reduce heat, and simmer 30 minutes. Stir in 1 cup sliced green onions, and remove from heat. Cool; package in 3 quart-size jars for gift giving. Chill up to 24 hours, and deliver with reheating instructions.
Yield: about 3 quarts chowder

Directions for gift card: Keep refrigerated until ready to serve, up to 24 hours. When ready to serve, cook chowder over low heat just until reheated.

Spiced Peach Jam, page 94;
Cranberry-Jalapeño Salsa, page 85;
Homemade Vanilla Extract, page 96

Sauces and Such

Start cooking a month or two before Christmas? You bet, with many of these sauces and condiments. From savory to sweet, these favorites are sure to please loved ones on your gift list.

Meat Sauce for Spaghetti

This recipe makes several gifts. Give a jar with a bag full of pasta and a loaf of bread for instant enjoyment.

- 5 pounds ground chuck
- 6 medium onions, diced
- 5 large ribs celery, diced
- 2 cans (28 ounces each) crushed tomatoes
- 2 cans (26 ounces each) tomato sauce
- 2 cans (12 ounces each) tomato paste
- 2 bottles (12 ounces each) chili sauce
- 2 cans (12 ounces each) sliced mushrooms, drained
- 4 cups water
- 3 to 4 tablespoons sugar
- 2 teaspoons salt
- 2 teaspoons coarsely ground pepper
- 2 teaspoons white vinegar

In an 8-quart stockpot, cook meat, onions, and celery over medium heat 8 to 10 minutes, stirring until beef crumbles and is no longer pink; drain well, and return to stockpot.

Add crushed tomatoes and remaining ingredients to stockpot; reduce heat to low, and cook, stirring often, 1 hour. Remove from heat, and cool.

Pour into hot sterilized jars. Store in refrigerator. **Yield:** about 7 quarts sauce

Directions for gift card: Refrigerate up to 3 days, or freeze sauce in heavy-duty resealable plastic bags up to 3 months. (Thaw in refrigerator when ready to heat and serve.)

Meat Sauce for Spaghetti, Caramel Sauce (page 98), Applesauce (page 98), Cumberland Sauce

Cumberland Sauce

This tangy-sweet sauce has great depth of flavor. Inform recipients on the gift tag that it's delicious with pork and turkey, and can be used as a glaze for ham.

- 2½ cups port wine, divided
- 1 jar (10½ ounces) red currant jelly
- 3 tablespoons light brown sugar
- 2 tablespoons grated orange zest
- ⅔ cup fresh orange juice
- 1½ tablespoons freshly grated ginger
- 2 teaspoons dry mustard
- ¼ teaspoon salt
- ¼ teaspoon ground red pepper
- 2½ tablespoons cornstarch

In a large saucepan, bring 2 cups wine and next 8 ingredients to a boil, stirring constantly; reduce heat, and simmer, stirring often, 20 minutes.

Stir together remaining ½ cup wine and cornstarch until smooth. Stir into hot mixture; bring to a boil over medium heat. Boil, stirring constantly, 1 minute. Remove from heat, and cool. Pour into hot sterilized jars, and seal. Chill.
Yield: about 4 cups sauce

Directions for gift card: Store in refrigerator up to 1 month.

Bourbon Glaze for Ham

Going to a friend's for Christmas dinner? Take this sweet glaze for an unforgettable accent.

- 1 cup honey
- ½ cup molasses
- ½ cup bourbon*
- ¼ cup orange juice
- 2 tablespoons Dijon mustard

In a 1-quart glass dish, microwave honey and molasses on high power (100%) for 1 minute. Whisk to blend. Whisk in bourbon, juice, and mustard. Cool, spoon into jars, and chill.
Yield: about 2¼ cups glaze

*Substitute ½ cup orange juice for bourbon, if desired.

Directions for gift card: Chill up to 1 week. Heat in microwave on high power (100%) for 1 minute. Brush warm sauce over ham the last 20 minutes it bakes, or serve warm on the side with ham.

Cranberry-Horseradish Sauce

Cranberry-Horseradish Sauce

A cute jar, bow, and greenery dress this zesty sauce for gift giving.

- 2 cups fresh cranberries
- 1 small onion, quartered
- ¾ cup sour cream
- ½ cup sugar
- 2 tablespoons prepared horseradish
- ½ teaspoon salt

Pulse cranberries and onion in a food processor until coarsely chopped, stopping to scrape down sides.

Stir together cranberry mixture, sour cream, and remaining 3 ingredients in a medium bowl. Spoon into jars, and chill.
Yield: about 2½ cups sauce

Directions for gift card: Store in an airtight container in refrigerator up to 4 days. Serve with roast beef, turkey, or as a sandwich spread.

Cider Vinegar Barbecue Sauce

This sauce is often referred to as Lexington-Style Dip, and there are many variations to this traditional Southern sauce. Package it along with a basting brush for grilling.

- 1½ cups cider vinegar
- ⅓ cup firmly packed brown sugar
- ¼ cup ketchup
- 1 tablespoon hot sauce
- 1 teaspoon browning and seasoning sauce
- ½ teaspoon salt
- ½ teaspoon onion powder
- ½ teaspoon pepper
- ½ teaspoon Worcestershire sauce

In a medium saucepan, stir together all ingredients; cook over medium heat, stirring constantly, 7 minutes or until sugar dissolves. Cover and chill.
Yield: about 2 cups sauce

Directions for gift card: Chill up to 2 weeks. Use as a basting sauce for pork or chicken.

Quick Fruited Salsa

This colorful salsa will liven up anything from grilled chicken to tortilla chips.

- 2 cans (11 ounces each) mandarin oranges, drained
- 1 can (8 ounces) pineapple tidbits in juice, drained
- 1 can (15 ounces) black beans, rinsed and drained
- 1 sweet red pepper, chopped
- ½ cup chopped red onion
- 1 tablespoon dried cilantro
- 2 tablespoons chopped canned jalapeño pepper
- 1 tablespoon lime juice
- ¼ teaspoon minced garlic

Drain oranges; let stand on several layers of paper towels to absorb excess moisture. Snip orange slices in half using kitchen shears.

Combine pineapple and remaining 7 ingredients in a medium bowl, mixing well. Add oranges, stirring gently to combine. Spoon mixture into wide-mouth jars; seal and refrigerate.
Yield: about 5 cups salsa

Directions for gift card: Chill up to 1 week. Serve as an appetizer with tortilla chips or as an accompaniment to chicken, fish, or pork.

Quick Fruited Salsa

Cranberry-Jalapeño Salsa

(pictured on page 80)

Holiday turkey or pork takes a lively twist with this jazzed-up cranberry sauce.

>   1 package (12 ounces) fresh cranberries
>   1 medium navel orange, unpeeled and coarsely
>   chopped
>   3 tablespoons crystallized ginger
>   2 jalapeño peppers, seeded and coarsely
>   chopped
> ¼ cup fresh mint leaves
>   1 cup sugar

   Pulse fresh cranberries in a food processor until minced. Transfer minced cranberries to a small bowl.
   Pulse orange and next 4 ingredients in food processor 3 to 5 times or until mixture is finely chopped. Stir into cranberries; cover and chill, if desired.
Yield: about 2 cups salsa

Directions for gift card: Chill up to 1 week. Serve with roast pork or turkey.

Cranberry-Ginger Chutney   Big Batch

This chutney will be a beloved favorite alongside pork or chicken. The tart cranberries mellow with the addition of sweet raisins and a touch of ginger.

>   1 package (12 ounces) fresh cranberries
> 1½ cups sugar
>   1 cup fresh orange juice
>   2 ribs celery, chopped
>   1 cup golden raisins
>   1 medium apple, chopped
>   1 tablespoon grated orange zest
>   1 teaspoon minced fresh ginger
>   1 cup chopped walnuts, toasted

   In a large saucepan, bring cranberries, sugar, and orange juice to a boil. Reduce heat, and simmer 15 minutes. Remove from heat.
   Stir in celery, raisins, apple, orange zest, and ginger. Stir in walnuts. Cool, spoon into gift jars, and chill.
Yield: about 6 cups chutney

Directions for gift card: Chill up to 1 week. Serve with roast pork or chicken.

Chowchow

Here's a gift you can make in the summer or fall when green tomatoes are available. This chunky condiment is canned and sealed by the traditional method, so it will keep up to a year in a cool, dry place. For more heat, add chopped jalapeño to the vegetables.

>   5 green peppers
>   5 sweet red peppers
>   2 large green tomatoes
>   2 large onions
> ½ small cabbage
> ¼ cup pickling salt
>   3 cups sugar
>   2 cups white vinegar (5% acidity)
>   1 cup water
>   1 tablespoon mustard seed
> 1½ teaspoons celery seed
> ¾ teaspoon ground turmeric

   Chop peppers, tomatoes, onions, and cabbage.
   Stir together chopped vegetables and salt in a large Dutch oven. Cover and chill 8 hours. Rinse and drain; return mixture to Dutch oven. Stir in sugar and remaining ingredients. Bring to a boil; reduce heat, and simmer 3 minutes.
   Pack hot mixture into hot jars, filling to ½ inch from top. Remove air bubbles; wipe jar rims. Cover at once with metal lids, and screw on bands.
   Process jars in boiling-water bath 15 minutes. Store in a cool, dry place.
Yield: about 5½ pints chowchow

Directions for gift card: Store in a cool, dry place. Once opened, refrigerate up to 2 weeks.

Sesame-Ginger Marinade

Sesame-Ginger Marinade

Package this marinade with grilling tools for the grill master on your gift list.

- ½ cup soy sauce
- ⅓ cup rice wine vinegar
- ⅓ cup canola oil
- ⅓ cup sesame oil
- 3 tablespoons honey
- 2 tablespoons minced fresh ginger
- 1 clove garlic, minced

Whisk together all ingredients until well blended. Cover and chill.
Yield: about 1½ cups marinade

Directions for gift card: Chill up to 1 week. Use for pork, chicken, or seafood.

Port Wine Marinade

Ice down a couple of rib-eyes alongside a bottle of this marinade for the beef lovers on your list.

- ½ cup port wine
- 1 tablespoon chopped fresh thyme leaves
- 3 tablespoons soy sauce
- ½ teaspoon pepper
- ½ teaspoon hot sauce
- 1 clove garlic, halved
- 1 bay leaf

In a small bowl, combine all ingredients; stir well. Cover and chill.
Yield: about ¾ cup marinade

Directions for gift card: Chill up to 1 week. Use to marinate beef, pork, or lamb.

Fresh Mint Vinegar

Select a bottle with artistic flair to give this vinegar in—when the bottle is empty, the recipient can wash it thoroughly and fill it with a favorite olive oil.

- 1 cup chopped fresh mint leaves
- 2 cups white wine vinegar

Place mint in a wide-mouth pint glass jar, and set aside. Pour vinegar into a non-aluminum saucepan; bring to a boil. Pour hot vinegar over mint in jar and cover with lid. Let stand at room temperature 2 weeks.
Pour mixture through a wire-mesh strainer lined with 2 layers of cheesecloth into a decorative bottle or jar, discarding mint. Seal bottle with a cork or an airtight lid.
Yield: about 2 cups vinegar

Directions for gift card: Use in vinaigrettes and in fruit or vegetable salads.

Spicy Southwest Chile Oil (following page), Fresh Mint Vinegar, Italian Herb Vinegar (following page)

Spicy Southwest Chile Oil

(pictured on previous page)

Pour this oil into a decorative bottle found at an antique store or flea market. Add chiles and top with a cork for a spicy gift.

    4 cloves garlic
    2 tablespoons white vinegar
    I jalapeño pepper
    I tablespoon coriander seed
    2 teaspoons cumin seed
    2 teaspoons dried oregano leaves
    2 cups extra virgin olive oil, divided
    2 green chile peppers, cut in half
    2 red chile peppers, cut in half

In a small glass bowl, combine garlic and vinegar; cover and refrigerate at least 8 hours. Drain garlic, discarding vinegar; rinse and pat dry with paper towels. Set garlic aside.

Remove stem from jalapeño pepper. Set pepper aside.

Heat a large skillet over medium heat 2 minutes; add coriander and cumin seed. Cook, stirring constantly, 5 minutes or until lightly browned.

Transfer browned seeds to container of an electric blender; add garlic, jalapeño pepper, oregano, and I cup oil. Cover and process until minced, stopping once to scrape down sides. Pour mixture into a jar; add remaining I cup oil. Cover and refrigerate 24 hours.

Let oil stand at room temperature 2 hours. Pour mixture through a wire-mesh strainer lined with 2 layers of cheesecloth into a decorative bottle or jar, discarding solids. Add chiles. Seal bottle with a cork or an airtight lid. Store in refrigerator.
Yield: about I ½ cups oil

Directions for gift card: Store in refrigerator up to I month. Use in salsas, fajitas, beans, and marinades for fish, or brush on vegetables before roasting.

Italian Herb Vinegar

(pictured on previous page)

Give this herbed vinegar in a simple corked bottle. Decorate the cork with colorful beads or ribbon for a lively touch.

    ½ cup chopped fresh oregano leaves
    ¼ cup chopped fresh rosemary
    ¼ cup chopped fresh basil leaves
    2 tablespoons chopped fresh sage
    I tablespoon chopped fresh parsley
    I tablespoon peppercorns
    I clove garlic, crushed
    4 cups red wine vinegar

Combine first 7 ingredients in a wide-mouth quart glass jar, and set aside. Pour vinegar into a non-aluminum saucepan; bring to a boil. Pour hot vinegar over herbs in jar; cover with lid. Let stand at room temperature 2 weeks.

Pour mixture through a wire-mesh strainer lined with 2 layers of cheesecloth into decorative bottles or jars, discarding herbs. Seal bottles with corks or airtight lids.
Yield: about 4 cups vinegar

Directions for gift card: Use in vinaigrettes, marinades, or vegetable salads.

Asian Vinaigrette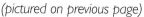

This simple and fast vinaigrette makes an elegant gift in a pretty bottle trimmed with a velvet ribbon and a sprig of greenery.

    ⅔ cup vegetable oil
    ½ cup rice vinegar
    ¼ cup hot sesame oil
    ¼ cup minced fresh ginger
    2 tablespoons lite soy sauce
    4 cloves garlic, minced
    I teaspoon freshly ground black pepper

Whisk together all ingredients. Pour vinaigrette into a decorative jar or bottle and seal with an airtight lid.
Yield: about I ½ cups vinaigrette

Directions for gift card: Store in refrigerator up to I month. Use to dress salad greens or vegetables.

Asian Vinaigrette

Apple Cider Vinaigrette

Package this tangy vinaigrette alongside a fruit basket for gift giving.

1½ cups vegetable oil
⅔ cup cider vinegar
⅔ cup firmly packed light brown sugar
2 teaspoons celery salt
1½ teaspoons dry mustard
3 tablespoons coarsely chopped onion

Process all ingredients in a blender or food processor until smooth. Package vinaigrette in an airtight container and chill.
Yield: about 2 cups vinaigrette

Directions for gift card: Store in refrigerator up to 1 month. Stir dressing well before drizzling desired amount over fresh fruit or spinach salad.

Basil-Honey Dressing

Give a bottle of this dressing with a pair of salad tongs decorated with a holiday bow.

½ cup white balsamic vinegar or white wine vinegar
½ cup honey
¼ cup vegetable oil
2 tablespoons chopped fresh basil leaves or 2 teaspoons dried basil leaves
½ teaspoon salt
½ teaspoon freshly ground black pepper

Combine all ingredients in a jar; cover tightly, and shake vigorously. Cover and chill.
Yield: about 1¼ cups dressing

Directions for gift card: Store in refrigerator up to 1 week. Serve with salad greens or grilled vegetables.

Oregano-Feta Dressing

Pair this dressing and a copy of the recipe with a salad spinner for infinite Greek salads.

6 ounces feta cheese, crumbled
½ cup buttermilk
6 tablespoons freshly squeezed lemon juice
1 tablespoon chopped fresh oregano leaves or 1 teaspoon dried oregano leaves
½ teaspoon freshly ground black pepper
¼ cup water
2 cloves garlic
¼ cup olive oil
½ small green pepper, chopped

In a food processor, process cheese, buttermilk, juice, oregano, pepper, water, and garlic until smooth. Gradually add oil in a steady stream, processing until smooth. Add green pepper, and pulse 3 seconds. Cover and chill.
Yield: about 2 cups dressing

Directions for gift card: Store in refrigerator up to 1 week. Use to dress salad greens, or sliced tomatoes or cucumbers.

Lime-Peanut Dressing

This Asian-inspired dressing looks great in a tall jar accented with a pair of chopsticks.

1 cup lime juice
6 tablespoons sugar
¼ cup finely chopped unsalted roasted peanuts
¼ cup fish sauce
2 tablespoons minced fresh ginger
2 tablespoons chopped fresh cilantro
8 cloves garlic, minced

In a medium bowl, stir together all ingredients until blended. Cover and chill.
Yield: about 2 cups dressing

Directions for gift card: Store in refrigerator up to 1 week. Serve dressing over mixed salad greens and assorted fresh vegetables.

Herbed Steak Rub

Herbed Steak Rub

Pack & Ship
Quick & Easy

This savory rub is the perfect gift for that steak lover who lives far away. Package it in resealable plastic bags that are easy to mail.

- 1/2 cup dried thyme leaves
- 1/2 cup dried basil leaves
- 1/2 cup dried rosemary leaves
- 2 1/2 tablespoons salt
- 2 1/2 tablespoons freshly ground black pepper
- 2 tablespoons ground red pepper

Combine all ingredients in a small bowl, and crush with the back of a spoon. Store in an airtight container. **Yield:** about 1 1/2 cups rub

Directions for gift card: Preheat oven to 400 degrees. Rub 1 to 1 1/2 teaspoons Herbed Steak Rub over a 6-ounce beef tenderloin steak, pork, or chicken. Brush an ovenproof skillet with 1 tablespoon olive oil, and place over medium-high heat until hot. Add steak, and cook 2 to 3 minutes on each side. Immediately place skillet in oven, and bake 8 to 10 minutes or until a meat thermometer inserted into thickest portion registers 145 degrees (medium-rare).

No-Sodium Creole Seasoning Blend

Most Creole seasonings are predominately salt, but this blend forgoes the salt and maximizes the ethnic flavors.

  3 tablespoons garlic powder
  3 tablespoons dried basil leaves
  3 tablespoons dried parsley flakes
  2 tablespoons onion powder
  5 teaspoons paprika
  4 teaspoons dry mustard
  2 teaspoons ground red pepper
  1 teaspoon freshly ground black pepper

In a small bowl, combine all ingredients; stir well. Store in an airtight container.
Yield: about 1 cup blend

Directions for gift card: Use to season chicken, dressings, dips, or vegetables. Shake well before each use.

Mexican Seasoning Blend

Give this Southwestern-seasoned blend with a bag of soft tortillas and a bottle of salsa—all the recipients need is the meat of their choice to make an instant fajita party.

  ½ cup chili powder
  ¼ cup paprika
  2 tablespoons ground cumin
  2 teaspoons garlic powder
  1 teaspoon ground red pepper
  ½ teaspoon salt

In a small bowl, combine all ingredients; stir well. Store in an airtight container.
Yield: about 1 cup blend

Directions for gift card: Use to season chicken, turkey, or beef. Shake well before each use.

Christmas Ambrosia

This tangy fruit mixture will delight every taste bud. Give it in an airtight jar along with a loaf of gingerbread.

  18 small oranges
  2 cans (15¼ ounces each) pineapple tidbits, undrained
  3 cups grated fresh, canned, or frozen coconut
  1 cup chopped walnuts, toasted

Peel and section oranges, catching juice in a large nonmetal bowl. Add orange sections, pineapple, coconut, and walnuts to juice; toss gently. Place in airtight containers. Cover and chill.
Yield: about 11 cups ambrosia

Directions for gift card: Store in refrigerator up to 4 days.

Easy Sweet-Tangy Mustard

Give this mustard with a spreader for instant enjoyment.

  1 can (14 ounces) sweetened condensed milk
  1 bottle (8 ounces) prepared mustard
  2 tablespoons prepared horseradish
  2 tablespoons Worcestershire sauce

Stir together milk, mustard, horseradish, and Worcestershire sauce until blended. Cover and chill.
Yield: about 3 cups mustard

Directions for gift card: Store in airtight jars in refrigerator up to 2 months. Serve with pretzels or egg rolls, or as a sandwich spread.

Easy Sweet-Tangy Mustard

Gingered Cinnamon Sugar

Gingered Cinnamon Sugar

The possibilities of this ginger-inspired sugar are endless. From breakfast to dessert pastries, there will be no problem thinking of a way to sweeten things up.

1 jar (2.7 ounces) crystallized ginger
1 cup sugar
1 cup firmly packed brown sugar
5 teaspoons ground cinnamon

Position knife blade in food processor bowl; add all ingredients. Process 1 minute or until mixture is a fine powder. Store in an airtight container in a cool, dark place.
Yield: about 2 cups sugar

Directions for gift card: Shake well before each use. Sprinkle on cinnamon toast or French toast or over hot cereal, bananas, broiled grapefruit, or baked apples or pears; stir into yogurt or sweet roll filling.

Citrus Marmalade

Spiced Peach Jam
(pictured on page 80)

This golden sweet jam stores in the refrigerator up to 1 month and makes 4 gifts using half-pint containers.

> 2 packages (16 ounces each) frozen sliced
>   peaches
> 1 package (16 ounces) light brown sugar
> ½ cup dry white wine
> ½ teaspoon salt
> ⅛ teaspoon freshly ground black pepper
> ⅛ teaspoon dried crushed red pepper
> ⅛ teaspoon ground cardamom
> ⅛ teaspoon ground ginger
> ⅛ teaspoon ground coriander
> ⅛ teaspoon ground cumin
> ⅛ teaspoon ground cinnamon
> ⅛ teaspoon ground cloves
> ½ cup chunky applesauce

In a large saucepan, bring peaches and brown sugar to a boil over medium heat; reduce heat, and simmer, stirring occasionally, 1 hour.

Stir in wine and next 9 ingredients. Cook, stirring occasionally, 45 minutes or until thickened. Cool slightly.

Process mixture in a food processor until smooth. Stir in applesauce. Spoon into hot sterilized jars; refrigerate.
Yield: about 4 cups jam

Directions for gift card: Store in refrigerator up to 1 month.

Citrus Marmalade

You'll be reminded of Grandma's citrus marmalade when making this recipe. It's a good thing one recipe makes several gifts, so you can keep one for yourself.

> 3 orange halves
> 2 lemon halves
> ½ grapefruit, peeled, seeded, and sectioned
> 6 cups sugar
> 4 cups water

Remove seeds from orange and lemon halves; coarsely chop rinds and pulp. Pulse orange, lemon, and grapefruit in a food processor 8 to 10 times or until fruit is finely chopped.

Cook fruit, sugar, and water in a heavy saucepan over medium heat, stirring constantly, until sugar dissolves. Cook, stirring often, 45 minutes to 1 hour until a candy thermometer registers 226 degrees.

Pack mixture into hot sterilized jars, filling to ¼ inch from top. Remove air bubbles; wipe jar rims. Cover at once with metal lids, and screw on bands.

Process jars in boiling-water bath 5 minutes.
Yield: about 8 half pints marmalade

Directions for gift card: Refrigerate up to 2 months after opening.

Honey-Lemon Jelly

The honey lover on your list will delight in this citrus-inspired version made into a pretty jelly.

> 5 or 6 lemons
> 2½ cups honey
> 1 package (3 ounces) liquid pectin

Grate zest from enough lemons to measure 4 teaspoons; set grated lemon zest aside.

Squeeze enough juice from lemons to measure ¾ cup; pour lemon juice through a wire-mesh strainer, discarding seeds and pulp. Combine grated zest, juice, and honey in a 6-quart saucepan, stirring well.

Bring mixture to a rolling boil over high heat, stirring constantly; quickly stir in pectin. Return to a rolling boil; boil 1 minute, stirring constantly. Remove from heat; skim off foam with a metal spoon.

Pour jelly quickly into hot, sterilized jars, filling to ¼ inch from top; wipe jar rims. Cover at once with metal lids, and screw on bands.

Process jars in boiling-water bath 5 minutes. Cool on wire racks. Store in a cool, dry place.
Yield: about 4 half pints jelly

Directions for gift card: Refrigerate up to 2 months after opening.

Cranberry Butter

Quick & Easy

This amazing butter makes a perfect gift for neighbors—it will leave their senses in awe. Enjoy this creamy delight for breakfast or as an afternoon snack with tea and scones.

1 cup butter, softened
½ cup sifted confectioners sugar
¼ cup whole berry cranberry sauce

Combine butter and confectioners sugar; beat at medium speed of an electric mixer until blended. Stir in cranberry sauce. Spoon mixture into a butter crock; cover and chill.
Yield: about 1½ cups butter

Directions for gift card: Store in refrigerator up to 2 weeks. Serve with waffles, pancakes, or scones.

Cranberry Butter and Ginger Scones (page 33)

Honey Butter

Spoon this sweet delight into a pretty container, and tie with a ribbon to give as a homespun hostess gift.

>   ½ cup butter, softened
>   ¼ cup honey
>   1 teaspoon grated orange zest
>   ½ teaspoon ground cinnamon

In a mixing bowl, combine butter, honey, orange zest, and cinnamon; beat at medium speed of an electric mixer until smooth. Store in refrigerator in an airtight container.
Yield: about ¾ cup butter

Directions for gift card: Store in refrigerator up to 2 weeks. Serve with bread, biscuits, English muffins, pancakes, waffles, or scones.

Homemade Vanilla Extract

(pictured on page 80)

Find small antique bottles at vintage and thrift stores to create a nostalgic gift from home.

>   6 vanilla beans, divided
>   1 quart vodka
>   1 cup sugar
>   ½ cup water

Cut each of 3 vanilla beans into 4 pieces; split each piece lengthwise. Place in a 1½-quart bottle, and add vodka. Cover tightly, and shake vigorously. Let stand in a cool, dry place 3 weeks, shaking bottle every 2 days.

Line a funnel with a coffee filter; pour mixture through funnel into a bowl, discarding beans.

Cook sugar and water in a small saucepan over medium-high heat, stirring occasionally, 2 to 3 minutes or until sugar dissolves. Remove from heat; cool completely. Add to vodka mixture.

Cut remaining 3 vanilla beans into pieces. Fill small bottles with 1 vanilla bean piece and extract; cover tightly, and let stand in a cool, dry place 1 month. Strain vanilla, discarding beans. Pour into decorative bottles.
Yield: about 4½ cups extract

Directions for gift card: Store at room temperature.

Zesty Lemon Sauce

Tie a zester onto the jar of lemon sauce, and attach a gift tag with instructions to "chill upon receiving." For an extra special gift, accompany with gingerbread or pound cake.

>   ¼ cup butter or margarine
>   2 tablespoons grated lemon zest
>   1 can (14 ounces) sweetened condensed milk
>   1 tablespoon freshly squeezed lemon juice

In a heavy saucepan, melt butter over low heat. Stir in lemon zest, and cook 2 minutes.

Whisk in sweetened condensed milk until smooth. Gradually add lemon juice, whisking constantly. Cool, and package into jars.
Yield: about 1½ cups sauce

Directions for gift card: Chill until ready to serve. Serve chilled, or heat in microwave just until warm, if desired. Serve over gingerbread or pound cake.

Stamped and Delivered

Stamps and ink pads (available at craft stores) are an inexpensive way to dress up gifts. You can stamp paper take-out containers, tissue paper, brown kraft paper, and boxes. Lightly press stamp on ink pad (too much ink will smear), then firmly press onto paper or boxes. You can even stamp a set of gift tags with ribbon ties to make a thoughtful gift.

Zesty Lemon Sauce

Applesauce

(pictured on page 82)

Just like mom used to make, this simple applesauce will bring childhood memories to any lucky recipient.

> 12 large Granny Smith apples, peeled and
>   coarsely chopped
> 1½ cups sugar
> ¼ cup freshly squeezed lemon juice

In a Dutch oven, cook apples, sugar, and lemon juice over low heat, stirring often, 10 minutes. (Sugar will dissolve and apples will begin to break down and release juices.) Increase heat to medium, and cook, stirring often, 25 minutes or until thickened. Spoon into hot sterilized jars, and seal. Chill.
Yield: about 6 cups applesauce

Directions for gift card: Store in refrigerator up to 1 month. Serve warm or cold.

Chocolate Fudge Sauce

Trim this gift with ribbon and an antique serving spoon.

> ¾ cup half and half
> 1½ cups semisweet chocolate morsels
> 1½ cups miniature marshmallows
> 1 teaspoon vanilla extract

In a heavy saucepan, heat half and half over medium-low heat. Stir in chocolate morsels and marshmallows. Cook over low heat, stirring constantly, until smooth. Remove from heat; stir in vanilla. Cool. Cover and chill.
Yield: about 2 cups sauce

Directions for gift card: Store in refrigerator up to 1 week. Microwave open container of sauce on medium power (50%) for 2 minutes or until thoroughly heated, stirring once. Serve over ice cream.

Safe Sauces

When delivering homemade sauces, be sure that your friends and relatives know to keep them cold. It's easy for a small gift to be lost in the holiday shuffle, so hand deliver yours, and mention that it needs to be stored in the refrigerator right away.

Caramel Sauce

(pictured on page 82)

This sweet sauce is great for serving warm over ice cream or chocolate cake. Attach a gift card to this package with instructions to warm the sauce briefly in the microwave before serving for best results.

> 1 cup butter
> 2 cups sugar
> 2 teaspoons freshly squeezed lemon juice
> 1½ cups whipping cream

In a heavy saucepan, melt butter over medium heat; add sugar and lemon juice, and cook, stirring constantly, 6 to 8 minutes or until mixture turns a deep caramel color. Gradually add cream, and cook, stirring constantly, 1 to 2 minutes or until smooth. Remove from heat, and cool. Pour into hot sterilized jars, and seal. Chill.
Yield: about 3 cups sauce

Directions for gift card: Store in refrigerator up to 1 month. Heat sauce briefly in the microwave before serving, if desired.

Praline Crunch Syrup

This New Orleans syrup will make your friends want to reminisce about the Crescent City.

> 1½ cups maple-flavored syrup
> ½ cup chopped toasted pecans (toasting
>   optional)
> 2 bars (1.4 ounces each) chocolate-covered
>   toffee, crushed

In a small bowl, combine syrup, pecans, and candy, stirring gently until blended. Using a wide-mouthed funnel, transfer to a bottle; seal.
Yield: about 2½ cups syrup

Directions for gift card: Store in refrigerator up to 1 week.

Lemon-Berry Syrup

This syrup is great served over pancakes. Give it along with a bag of Hearty Cornmeal Pancake Mix (page 42).

- 1 cup strawberry jam
- ½ cup frozen lemonade concentrate, thawed and undiluted
- 1 cup frozen blueberries

In a small bowl, combine jam, lemonade concentrate, and blueberries, stirring gently until blended. Using a wide-mouthed funnel, transfer syrup to a bottle; seal. Store in refrigerator.
Yield: about 2½ cups syrup

Directions for gift card: Store in refrigerator up to 1 week. Use to top pancakes, pound cake, or ice cream.

Georgia Peach Honey

This honey and homemade biscuits are a match made in heaven. Package them together for a fuss-free homestyle breakfast.

- 1 cup honey
- ¾ cup peach jam
- ¼ cup orange juice

In a medium bowl, combine honey, jam, and juice, stirring until blended. Using a wide-mouthed funnel, transfer to a bottle; seal. Store in refrigerator.
Yield: about 2 cups honey

Directions for gift card: Store in refrigerator up to 1 week.

Praline Crunch Syrup, Lemon-Berry Syrup, Georgia Peach Honey

Raspberry-Fudge Truffles, page 126;
Lemon Butter Cookies, page 118;
Turtle Cookies, page 117

Sugar & Spice

Cookies and candies are
favorite sweets for young and
old alike. Most of these recipes
make enough for several
batches, so they'll make
your time in the kitchen
more efficient. They're easy to
make and even easier to give!

Orange-Macadamia Nut Cookies, Fudgy Joy Cookies, Two-Tone Cookies

Fudgy Joy Cookies

Soft, chocolaty cookies still warm from the oven are always a big hit. This recipe will remind you of a popular coconut-almond-chocolate candy bar.

    2 cups all-purpose flour
    ½ cup quick-cooking oats
    ½ cup cocoa
    1 teaspoon baking soda
    ¼ teaspoon salt
    1 cup butter or margarine
    3 squares (1 ounce each) semisweet chocolate,
         finely chopped
    1 cup granulated sugar
    ½ cup firmly packed brown sugar
    2 eggs
    2 teaspoons vanilla extract
    ¾ cup finely chopped flaked coconut
    ½ cup slivered almonds, toasted and coarsely
         chopped

In a medium bowl, combine flour, oats, cocoa, baking soda, and salt; stir well, and set aside.

Combine butter and chocolate in a small saucepan; cook over low heat, stirring often, until melted and smooth. Remove from heat. Transfer mixture to a large bowl; cool completely.

Add sugars to chocolate mixture, beating at medium speed of an electric mixer until well blended. Add eggs and vanilla; beat until smooth. Gradually add flour mixture, beating well. Stir in coconut and almonds. Cover and chill dough 1 hour.

Preheat oven to 350 degrees. Drop dough by rounded tablespoonfuls onto ungreased baking sheets. Bake 10 minutes. Cool 1 minute on baking sheets; remove to wire racks, and cool completely.

Yield: about 3½ dozen cookies

Two-Tone Cookies: Preheat oven to 350 degrees. Fill half of a measuring tablespoon with Fudgy Joy Cookie dough. Press Orange-Macadamia Nut Cookie dough into the other half of spoon. Drop two-toned dough onto ungreased baking sheets. Repeat procedure with remaining dough. Bake 10 to 12 minutes. Cool 2 minutes on baking sheets; remove to wire racks, and cool completely.

Yield: about 6 dozen cookies

Heavenly Chocolate Chunk Cookies

Mega-morsels give a big chocolate taste to every bite of these deluxe chocolate chip cookies.

   2 cups plus 2 tablespoons all-purpose flour
½ teaspoon baking soda
½ teaspoon salt
¾ cup butter or margarine
   2 tablespoons instant coffee granules
   I cup firmly packed brown sugar
½ cup granulated sugar
   I egg
   I egg yolk
   I package (11.5 ounces) semisweet chocolate
       mega-morsels
   I cup walnut halves, toasted

Preheat oven to 325 degrees. In a medium bowl, combine flour, baking soda, and salt; stir well.

Combine butter and coffee granules in a small saucepan or skillet. Cook over medium-low heat until butter melts and coffee granules dissolve, stirring occasionally. Remove from heat, and cool to room temperature. (Don't let butter resolidify.)

Combine butter mixture, sugars, egg, and egg yolk in a large bowl. Beat at medium speed of an electric mixer until blended. Gradually add flour mixture, beating at low speed just until blended. Stir in mega-morsels and walnuts.

Drop dough by heaping tablespoonfuls 2 inches apart onto ungreased baking sheets. Bake 12 to 14 minutes. Cool slightly on baking sheets. Remove to wire racks, and cool completely.

Yield: about 20 cookies

Heavenly Chocolate Chunk Cookies

Orange-Macadamia Nut Cookies

Macadamia nuts and white chocolate pair up in this delicious drop cookie. You can substitute other kinds of nuts, if you prefer.

¾ cup butter or margarine, softened
½ cup granulated sugar
½ cup firmly packed brown sugar
   I egg
   I tablespoon grated orange zest
¾ teaspoon vanilla extract
¼ teaspoon orange extract
I⅓ cups all-purpose flour
½ cup quick-cooking oats
¾ teaspoon baking powder
½ teaspoon baking soda
   I jar (3.5 ounces) lightly salted macadamia nuts,
       coarsely chopped
   I cup white chocolate morsels or chunks

Beat butter at medium speed of an electric mixer 2 minutes or until creamy. Gradually add sugars, beating well. Add egg, orange zest, vanilla, and orange extract.

Combine flour, oats, baking powder, and baking soda. Add to butter mixture, beating at low speed just until blended. Stir in nuts and white chocolate morsels. Cover and chill dough 2 hours.

Preheat oven to 350 degrees. Drop dough by rounded tablespoonfuls onto ungreased baking sheets. Bake 9 to 10 minutes or just until edges are golden. Cool 1 minute on baking sheets; remove to wire racks, and cool completely.

Yield: about 3 dozen cookies

Buttercrisp Cookies

These crispy-edged cookies have bits of candy in every bite. Bake on parchment paper to easily remove cookies to wire racks.

> ¾ cup unsalted butter, softened
> ¾ cup granulated sugar
> ¾ cup firmly packed brown sugar
> 2 eggs
> 2¼ cups all-purpose flour
> 2 teaspoons baking powder
> 1 teaspoon salt
> 1 tablespoon vanilla extract
> 1 package (6 ounces) white chocolate baking squares, coarsely chopped
> 6 bars (2.1 ounces each) chocolate-covered crispy peanut-buttery candy, coarsely chopped
> 1 cup uncooked regular oats

Beat butter at medium speed of an electric mixer until creamy. Add sugars, beating until fluffy. Add eggs, 1 at a time, beating just until blended.

Combine flour, baking powder, and salt. Gradually add to butter mixture, beating until blended. Stir in vanilla. Stir in white chocolate, candy, and oats. Cover and chill dough 30 minutes.

Preheat oven to 350 degrees. Drop dough by heaping teaspoonfuls onto parchment paper-lined baking sheets. Bake 8 to 9 minutes or until golden. (Do not overbake.) Cool 5 minutes on baking sheets; remove to wire racks, and cool completely.

Yield: about 5 dozen cookies

Triple Chocolate Chubbies

Three and a half dozen of these triple chocolate cookies host a full 6 cups of nuts and chocolate morsels. No wonder they're called chubbies.

> 6 squares (1 ounce each) semisweet chocolate, chopped
> 2 squares (1 ounce each) unsweetened chocolate, chopped
> ⅓ cup butter or margarine
> 3 eggs
> 1 cup sugar
> ¼ cup all-purpose flour
> ½ teaspoon baking powder
> ⅛ teaspoon salt
> 2 cups (12 ounces) semisweet chocolate morsels
> 2 cups coarsely chopped pecans
> 2 cups coarsely chopped walnuts

Preheat oven to 325 degrees. In a heavy saucepan, combine chocolate squares and butter; cook, stirring often, over low heat until chocolate melts. Remove from heat; cool slightly.

Beat eggs and sugar at medium speed of an electric mixer until smooth; add chocolate mixture, beating well.

Combine flour, baking powder, and salt; add to chocolate mixture, stirring just until dry ingredients are moistened. Fold in chocolate morsels, pecans, and walnuts.

Drop batter by tablespoonfuls 2 inches apart onto lightly greased baking sheets. Bake 12 to 15 minutes or until done. Cool cookies on baking sheets 1 minute. Remove to wire racks, and cool completely.

Yield: about 3½ dozen cookies

Chocolate-Chocolate Chip-Peppermint Cookies

Crushed peppermint candy stirred into the batter dresses these chocolate chippers for the holidays. Tie a giant candy cane to the side of a gift basket of the cookies for a festive adornment.

> ¼ cup butter or margarine, softened
> ¼ cup vegetable shortening
> 1½ cups firmly packed brown sugar
> ½ cup granulated sugar
> 2 eggs
> 1½ teaspoons vanilla extract
> 1¾ cups all-purpose flour
> 1 teaspoon baking soda
> ¾ teaspoon salt
> ¼ cup cocoa
> ¾ cup semisweet chocolate morsels
> ¾ cup coarsely crushed peppermint candy (about 8 large candy canes)

Preheat oven to 350 degrees. Beat butter and shortening at medium speed of an electric mixer until creamy; gradually add sugars to creamed mixture, beating well.

Add eggs, 1 at a time, beating until blended after each addition. Stir in vanilla.

Combine flour, baking soda, salt, and cocoa; add flour mixture to butter mixture, beating until blended.

Fold in semisweet chocolate morsels and crushed peppermint candy.

Drop dough by rounded tablespoonfuls 3 inches apart onto lightly greased baking sheets. Bake 12 to 14 minutes. (Do not overbake.) Remove cookies to wire racks, and cool completely.

Yield: about 2½ dozen cookies

Coffee Bean Cookies

Big Batch

For the coffee lover on your list, these drop cookies are studded with chocolate-covered coffee beans, chunks of toffee candy bars, and almonds.

½ cup butter or margarine, softened
½ cup vegetable shortening
¾ cup granulated sugar
¾ cup firmly packed brown sugar
2 eggs
1 teaspoon vanilla extract
2¼ cups all-purpose flour
1 teaspoon baking soda
1 teaspoon salt
½ teaspoon ground cinnamon
1 cup chopped almonds, toasted
3 packages (2 ounces each) chocolate-covered coffee beans
4 bars (1.4 ounces each) English toffee-flavored candy, chopped

Preheat oven to 350 degrees. Beat butter and shortening at medium speed of an electric mixer until creamy; gradually add sugars, beating well. Add eggs and vanilla; beat well.

Combine flour, baking soda, salt, and cinnamon; add to butter mixture, beating well. Stir in almonds, coffee beans, and candy. Cover and chill dough, if desired.

Drop dough by heaping teaspoonfuls onto ungreased baking sheets. Bake 10 to 11 minutes or until golden. Cool on baking sheets 1 minute; remove to wire racks, and cool completely.

Yield: about 4 dozen cookies

Coffee Bean Cookies

Chocolate Cappuccino Cookies

These gourmet cookies make enough for two or three gifts for coffee connoisseurs. Package them with a pound of premium coffee beans for an extraspecial gift.

    2 cups butter or margarine, softened
    4 cups firmly packed light brown sugar
    4 eggs
5½ cups all-purpose flour
    1 cup cocoa
    ¼ cup instant coffee granules
    1 teaspoon baking powder
    1 teaspoon baking soda
    1 teaspoon salt
    1 package (10 ounces) cinnamon chips

Preheat oven to 350 degrees. Beat butter at medium speed of an electric mixer until creamy. Gradually add brown sugar, beating well. Add eggs, beating until blended.

Combine flour and next 5 ingredients. Gradually add to butter mixture, beating at low speed just until blended. Stir in cinnamon chips.

Drop dough by rounded tablespoonfuls 2 inches apart onto lightly greased baking sheets. Bake 8 to 10 minutes. Cool on baking sheets 5 minutes. Remove to wire racks, and cool completely.
Yield: about 8 dozen cookies

White Christmas Tropical Macaroons

You'll receive rave reviews for these white chocolate-infused macaroons full of dried pineapple and macadamia nuts.

    4 ounces white chocolate, coarsely chopped
    1 cup sugar
    ¼ teaspoon ground ginger
    ¼ teaspoon ground cinnamon
    4 egg whites
    2 cups flaked coconut
    1 cup finely chopped dried pineapple
    ½ cup finely chopped macadamia nuts or pecans

Preheat oven to 350 degrees. In a small glass bowl, microwave chopped white chocolate on high power (100%) for 1½ minutes or until melted, stirring once. Set aside.

Stir together sugar, ginger, and cinnamon.

Beat egg whites at high speed of an electric mixer until foamy. Add sugar mixture, 1 tablespoon at a time, beating until stiff peaks form and sugar dissolves (2 to 4 minutes). Fold in white chocolate, coconut, pineapple, and macadamia nuts.

Drop mixture by rounded tablespoonfuls 2 inches apart onto parchment paper-lined baking sheets. Bake 13 to 17 minutes or until edges begin to brown. Remove to wire racks, and cool completely.
Yield: about 4 dozen cookies

Cranberry-Almond Cookies

Fresh cranberries add nice color and lots of tang to these almond sugar cookies that will make you famous among whomever you share them with.

    1 cup butter or margarine, softened
    ¾ cup granulated sugar
    ¾ cup firmly packed light brown sugar
    ½ teaspoon almond extract
    2 eggs
2¼ cups all-purpose flour
    1 teaspoon baking powder
    1 teaspoon salt
    2 cups chopped fresh cranberries
    1 cup slivered almonds, toasted

Preheat oven to 375 degrees. Beat butter at medium speed of an electric mixer until creamy; gradually add sugars, beating well. Add almond extract and eggs, beating until blended.

Combine flour, baking powder, and salt; gradually add to butter mixture, beating at low speed until blended after each addition. Stir in cranberries and almonds.

Drop by rounded tablespoonfuls onto ungreased baking sheets. Bake 9 to 11 minutes. Remove to wire racks, and cool completely.
Yield: about 3½ dozen cookies

The Scoop on Cookies

Making several dozen cookies a uniform size can sometimes be a challenge. And the yield of some cookie recipes may be altered when cookies aren't consistent in size. But you can easily make drop cookies the same size time after time. Whenever a recipe calls for dropping the dough by tablespoonfuls, use a cookie scoop instead of the traditional tablespoon. Cookie scoops come in several different sizes to suit your desired cookie size, so start scooping your way to uniform cookies.

Chocolate-Apricot Thumbprint Cookies

Pockets of apricot preserves fill these pecan-coated cookies. A chocolate drizzle dresses them up, but they're just as tempting unadorned. See how we stacked them for gift giving on page 185.

½ cup butter or margarine, softened
½ cup sugar
1 egg, separated
1 teaspoon vanilla extract
1 cup all-purpose flour
¼ teaspoon salt
2 cups finely chopped pecans, divided
½ cup apricot preserves
½ cup semisweet chocolate morsels, melted

Beat butter at medium speed of an electric mixer until creamy; gradually add sugar, beating until fluffy. Add egg yolk and vanilla; beat well.

Combine flour and salt; add to butter mixture, beating well. Stir in 1 cup pecans. Cover and chill dough at least 30 minutes.

Preheat oven to 350 degrees. Lightly beat egg white. Shape dough into 1-inch balls; dip each ball in egg white, and roll in remaining 1 cup pecans. Place balls 1 inch apart on greased baking sheets. Press thumb gently into center of each ball, leaving an indention; fill with preserves.

Bake 17 to 18 minutes or until lightly browned. Cool 1 minute on baking sheets; remove to wire racks, and cool completely. Drizzle melted chocolate over cooled cookies, using a fork or spoon.
Yield: about 3 dozen cookies

Chocolate-Apricot Thumbprint Cookies

Peppermint Cookie Canes

It's easy to fashion these shapely cookie candy canes. Just twist small ropes of colored dough together and shape into a cane. They'll harden up after cooling.

½ cup butter or margarine, softened
½ cup butter-flavored vegetable shortening or regular vegetable shortening
1½ cups sugar
1 egg
1½ teaspoons peppermint extract
½ teaspoon vanilla extract
3½ cups sifted cake flour
1½ teaspoons baking powder
¼ teaspoon salt
¾ teaspoon red paste food coloring

Beat butter and shortening at medium speed of an electric mixer until creamy; gradually add sugar, beating well. Add egg, beating well. Stir in flavorings. Combine flour, baking powder, and salt; add to butter mixture, beating well. Remove half of dough from bowl. Add food coloring to dough in bowl, and mix until color is evenly distributed.

Working with half of each dough at a time, shape plain dough by teaspoonfuls into 4-inch ropes. (Cover remaining dough to prevent drying.) Repeat shaping with red dough. Place one red rope and one plain rope side by side; carefully twist together. Roll twisted ropes into one smooth rope; shape rope into a cane, and twist as needed to complete stripe design. Repeat with remaining dough. Chill 15 minutes.

Preheat oven to 375 degrees. Place cookie canes on ungreased baking sheets. Bake 8 minutes or just until cookies begin to brown. Cool slightly; carefully remove cookies to wire racks, using a wide spatula, and cool completely.
Yield: about 4 dozen cookies

Chunky Peanut Butter Cookies

Here's a great cookie made of nutritious ingredients for friends who try to eat healthfully. Peanut butter and wheat germ lace this chunky cookie with rich nutrients.

1 cup extra-crunchy peanut butter
¾ cup firmly packed brown sugar
½ cup butter or margarine, softened
¼ cup honey
½ teaspoon vanilla extract
1 egg
1½ cups all-purpose flour
½ teaspoon baking soda
½ teaspoon salt
½ cup wheat germ

Preheat oven to 325 degrees. Beat peanut butter, brown sugar, butter, honey, vanilla, and egg at medium speed of an electric mixer until creamy. Combine flour and remaining 3 ingredients. Gradually add to butter mixture, beating well.

Shape dough into 1-inch balls. Place 2 inches apart on ungreased baking sheets. Flatten cookie balls with the back of a fork, forming a crisscross pattern. Bake 12 minutes or until lightly browned. Cool 1 minute on baking sheets; remove to wire racks, and cool completely.
Yield: about 4 dozen cookies

Snowball Sandwich Cookies

The only cooking you have to do to make these snowy gems is to melt white chocolate. Just sandwich store-bought wedding cookies together with the melted chocolate, and let them harden. Package the sandwich cookies in clever waxed paper-wrapped bakery boxes. You can find 5-inch boxes like we used in the photograph at your local bakery.

6 ounces white chocolate, chopped
2 bags (12 ounces each) wedding cookies

Place white chocolate in top of a double boiler; bring water to a boil. Reduce heat to low; cook until chocolate melts, stirring occasionally. Dip bottoms (flat sides) of half the cookies in white chocolate; press flat sides of remaining cookies against dipped cookies, creating sandwiches. Place on wire racks; let stand until white chocolate filling is firm.

Divide cookies into four portions. Pack each portion in a medium-size resealable plastic bag. Place each bag in a bakery box.
Yield: about 4 dozen cookies

Snowball Sandwich Cookies

Ready-to-Bake Double Chocolate Chip Cookies

A tub of this homemade cookie dough makes a welcome gift at this busy time of year.

- 1 cup butter or margarine, softened
- 1 cup granulated sugar
- 1 cup firmly packed brown sugar
- 2 eggs
- ½ teaspoon vanilla extract
- 2½ cups old-fashioned oats
- 2 cups all-purpose flour
- 1 teaspoon baking powder
- 1 teaspoon baking soda
- ½ teaspoon salt
- 3 bars (1.55 ounces each) milk chocolate candy, coarsely chopped
- 1½ cups chopped pecans
- 1 package (12 ounces) semisweet chocolate chips

In a large bowl, cream butter and sugars at medium speed of an electric mixer until fluffy. Add eggs and vanilla; beat until smooth. Process oats in a food processor until finely ground. Add flour and next 3 ingredients. Process until well blended. Add dry ingredients to butter mixture; stir until a soft dough forms. Stir in chopped candy bars, pecans, and chocolate chips. Spoon into an airtight container, and chill.
Yield: dough for about 5 dozen cookies

Directions for gift card: Store cookie dough in an airtight container in refrigerator up to 3 days. Preheat oven to 375 degrees. Drop teaspoonfuls of dough 2 inches apart onto lightly greased baking sheets. Bake 12 minutes or until bottoms of cookies are lightly browned. Cool 2 minutes on baking sheets; transfer cookies to wire racks, and cool completely.
Yield: about 5 dozen cookies

Graham Cracker Layered Cookies

These scrumptious bar cookies fit perfectly in one layer inside a shallow box. Just wrap the top and bottom of the box separately in wrapping paper and trim with a bow.

- 1 package (16 ounces) graham crackers, divided
- 1 cup butter or margarine
- 1 cup granulated sugar
- 1 egg
- 1¼ cups evaporated milk, divided
- 1½ cups chopped pecans, toasted and divided
- 1 cup flaked coconut
- 1 teaspoon vanilla extract
- 2 cups confectioners sugar
- 6 tablespoons butter or margarine, melted

Crush 7 whole graham crackers; set aside.
Arrange 8 whole graham crackers in bottom of a lightly greased 9 x 13-inch pan.
Melt 1 cup butter in a heavy saucepan; whisk in 1 cup sugar, egg, and 1 cup evaporated milk. Bring to a boil over medium heat, whisking constantly. Remove from heat.
Stir in crushed graham crackers, 1 cup pecans, coconut, and vanilla. Pour over crackers in pan. Arrange 8 whole graham crackers over top.
Stir together confectioners sugar, 6 tablespoons butter, and remaining ¼ cup evaporated milk until smooth.
Pour over graham cracker layer, and sprinkle with remaining ½ cup pecans. Cover; chill 4 hours. Cut into squares. Store in refrigerator, or freeze up to 1 month.
Yield: about 4 dozen cookies

Chocolate Graham Cracker Layered Cookies: Stir 1 cup (6 ounces) semisweet chocolate morsels into coconut mixture.

Raw Cookie Dough Dilemma

Nibbling on raw cookie dough has always been a favorite pastime among children. But if the dough contains raw eggs, the great taste comes with great risk.

Uncooked eggs carry the risk of salmonella contamination, which can cause illness. So be sure to bake the cookies before nibbling. Commercial cookie dough is made with pasteurized eggs, so it is safe to eat raw.

Graham Cracker Layered Cookies

Cherry Surprise Balls

Place the balls inside a red or green tin layered with tissue paper—this will hint of the colorful cherries hidden inside the cookies.

  ¾ cup butter or margarine, softened
  ½ cup confectioners sugar
  2 cups sifted cake flour
  1 teaspoon vanilla extract
  ½ cup chopped pecans
  14 red or green candied cherries, cut in half
      Confectioners sugar

Beat butter at medium speed of an electric mixer until creamy; gradually add confectioners sugar, beating well. Gradually add flour, beating until blended. Stir in vanilla and pecans. Cover and chill 1 hour.

Preheat oven to 375 degrees. Shape dough around each cherry half to form a ¾-inch ball. Place balls 2 inches apart on ungreased baking sheets.

Bake 20 minutes. Roll in confectioners sugar while warm. Cool on wire racks.
Yield: about 28 cookies

Pound Cake Cookies

Once you taste these buttery gems, you'll agree that they're a hands-down winner for holiday gift giving.

  1 cup butter, softened
  1 cup sugar
  1 egg yolk
  1 teaspoon rum or ½ teaspoon rum flavoring
  ½ teaspoon vanilla extract
  2¼ cups sifted cake flour
  ½ teaspoon salt
      About 42 pecan halves

Beat butter at medium speed of an electric mixer until creamy; gradually add sugar, beating well. Add egg yolk, rum, and vanilla; beat well. Combine flour and salt in a bowl; gradually add to butter mixture, beating well. Cover and chill at least 2 hours or until firm.

Preheat oven to 350 degrees. Shape dough into 1-inch balls; place 2 inches apart on ungreased baking sheets. Press one pecan half into each cookie.

Bake 12 to 14 minutes or until edges are lightly browned. Cool 2 minutes on baking sheets; remove to wire racks, and cool completely.
Yield: about 3½ dozen cookies

Ginger-Oatmeal Sorghum Cookies

These cookies offer old-fashioned goodness to the core, from their generous size to the oats and sorghum that flavor them.

  4 cups all-purpose flour
  1 tablespoon baking soda
  1½ teaspoons salt
  4 cups quick-cooking oats
  1¼ cups sugar
  1½ teaspoons ground ginger
  1½ cups raisins
  1 cup butter or margarine, melted
  1 cup sorghum
  1 cup chopped walnuts
  2 tablespoons hot water
  2 eggs, lightly beaten
  1 to 2 tablespoons water
  ½ cup sugar

Preheat oven to 375 degrees. In a large bowl, combine first 7 ingredients; add butter and next 4 ingredients, stirring until blended.

Shape dough into 36 (2½-inch) balls. Place 2 inches apart on lightly greased baking sheets; flatten each to ¼-inch thickness. Brush tops with 1 to 2 tablespoons water, and sprinkle with sugar. Bake 8 to 10 minutes or until lightly browned. Transfer to wire racks, and cool completely.
Yield: about 3 dozen cookies

Ginger-Oatmeal Sorghum Cookies

Crème de Menthe Bars

Crème de Menthe Bars

Rich, moist, and luscious layers flavored with chocolate syrup and mint inspired our staff to give these bars our highest rating.

½ cup butter or margarine, softened
1 cup granulated sugar
4 eggs
1 teaspoon vanilla extract
1 cup all-purpose flour
½ teaspoon salt
1 can (16 ounces) chocolate syrup
½ cup chopped pecans
½ cup butter or margarine, softened
2 cups confectioners sugar
1 to 1½ tablespoons crème de menthe
1 cup (6 ounces) semisweet chocolate morsels
6 tablespoons butter or margarine

Preheat oven to 350 degrees. Beat ½ cup butter at medium speed of an electric mixer until creamy; add 1 cup sugar, beating well. Add eggs and vanilla; beat well.

Combine flour and salt; add to butter mixture, beating mixture well. Stir in chocolate syrup and pecans. Pour batter into a greased 9 x 13-inch pan. Bake 35 minutes. Cool completely in pan on a wire rack.

Beat ½ cup butter at medium speed until creamy; add confectioners sugar and crème de menthe, beating until smooth. Spread over cooled brownie layer.

Combine chocolate morsels and 6 tablespoons butter in a small heavy saucepan over low heat, stirring until smooth. Cool 5 minutes, and spread over crème de menthe layer. Cover and chill at least 1 hour. Cut into bars.

Yield: about 2 dozen bars

Frosted Peanut Butter Brownies

Big Batch

Find fun-shaped boxes at any craft store to package these brownies in Christmas style.

1½ cups butter or margarine, divided
⅓ cup cocoa
2 cups granulated sugar
1½ cups all-purpose flour
½ teaspoon salt
4 eggs
1 teaspoon vanilla extract
1 jar (18 ounces) crunchy peanut butter
⅓ cup milk
10 large marshmallows
¼ cup cocoa
1 package (16 ounces) confectioners sugar

Preheat oven to 350 degrees. In a saucepan, cook 1 cup butter and ⅓ cup cocoa over low heat until butter melts, stirring often. Remove from heat, and cool slightly.

Combine sugar, flour, and salt in a large mixing bowl. Add chocolate mixture, and beat at medium speed of an electric mixer until blended. Add eggs and vanilla, beating until blended. Spread mixture into a greased and floured 10 x 15-inch jellyroll pan.

Bake 25 minutes or until a wooden pick inserted in center comes out clean.

Remove lid from peanut butter jar; microwave peanut butter on medium power (50%) for 2 minutes, stirring once. Spread over warm brownies. Chill 30 minutes.

Cook remaining ½ cup butter, milk, and marshmallows in a large saucepan over medium heat, stirring often, until marshmallows melt. Remove from heat, and whisk in ¼ cup cocoa. Gradually stir in confectioners sugar until smooth. Spread over peanut butter; chill 20 minutes. Cut into squares.
Yield: about 6 dozen brownies

Frosted Peanut Butter Brownies

Hazelnut Tile Brownies

These luscious brownies get a double dose of hazelnut flavor, first from chopped nuts in the crust and then from Frangelico, hazelnut liqueur that you splash into the batter. Rows of milk chocolate squares added after baking resemble rows of tile. The brownies don't stack well with their decorative top, so package them in a single layer.

      Hazelnut Crust
- ½ cup butter or margarine
- 4 squares (1 ounce each) semisweet chocolate, finely chopped
- ½ cup all-purpose flour
- ⅛ teaspoon salt
- 2 eggs
- ⅔ cup sugar
- 1 teaspoon vanilla extract
- 2 tablespoons Frangelico
- 16 squares (⅜ ounce each) milk chocolate
  Finely chopped hazelnuts, toasted

Prepare Hazelnut Crust; set aside.

In a small saucepan, combine butter and semisweet chocolate; place over medium-low heat. Cook until chocolate and butter melt, stirring until smooth. Cool 10 minutes.

Preheat oven to 350 degrees. Combine flour and salt; stir well, and set aside.

Combine eggs and sugar in a mixing bowl, and beat at medium-high speed of an electric mixer 3 minutes or until thick and pale. Add cooled chocolate mixture and vanilla; beat well. Add flour mixture, stirring well. Stir in Frangelico.

Pour chocolate batter over crust. Bake 32 minutes. (Top will appear cracked.) Place pan on a wire rack. Immediately arrange milk chocolate squares in rows over uncut brownies. Sprinkle with hazelnuts. The heat of the brownies will partially melt the chocolate squares, helping them to "frost" the brownies and hold the nuts on top. Cool and cut into 16 squares.

Yield: 16 brownies

Hazelnut Crust

- 1 package (2.25 ounces) chopped hazelnuts, toasted
- 1 cup all-purpose flour
  Pinch of salt
- ½ cup butter or margarine, cut up and softened
- ⅓ cup confectioners sugar

Preheat oven to 350 degrees. Line an 8-inch square pan with aluminum foil; grease foil.

Process hazelnuts, flour, and salt in a food processor 5 seconds or until nuts are finely chopped. Add butter and confectioners sugar; pulse until ingredients are combined. Press mixture into pan. Bake 12 minutes; cool.

Yield: 1 (8-inch) crust

Chocolate-Glazed Brownies

This brownie glaze is even easier than using canned frosting—just sprinkle chocolate morsels over the top and let them stand 5 minutes to soften. Then spread the melted chocolate with a spatula.

- 1 cup sugar
- ⅔ cup butter or margarine
- ¼ cup water
- 4 cups semisweet chocolate morsels, divided
- 1 teaspoon vanilla extract
- 1½ cups all-purpose flour
- ½ teaspoon baking soda
- ½ teaspoon salt
- 4 eggs
- 1 cup chopped pecans, toasted

In a large saucepan, cook sugar, butter, and water over high heat, stirring constantly, until sugar melts. Add 2 cups chocolate morsels and vanilla, stirring until mixture is smooth. Cool 15 minutes.

Preheat oven to 325 degrees. Add flour, baking soda, and salt to cooled chocolate mixture, stirring until blended; stir in eggs and chopped pecans until blended. Spread brownie batter into a greased and floured 9 x 13-inch pan.

Bake 30 minutes. Sprinkle remaining 2 cups chocolate morsels evenly over warm brownies, and let stand 5 minutes to soften. Spread over top. Transfer to a wire rack, and cool completely. Cut into bars.

Yield: about 18 brownies

Pecan Pie Bars, Pistachio Brittle (page 129)

Pecan Pie Bars

Pecan pie takes a turn as a bar cookie—and a rich one at that.

> 2 cups all-purpose flour
> ½ cup granulated sugar
> ⅛ teaspoon salt
> ¾ cup butter or margarine, cut up
> 1 cup firmly packed brown sugar
> 1 cup light corn syrup
> ½ cup butter or margarine
> 4 eggs, lightly beaten
> 2½ cups finely chopped pecans
> 1 teaspoon vanilla extract

Preheat oven to 350 degrees. In a large bowl, combine flour, sugar, and salt; cut in ¾ cup butter thoroughly with a pastry blender until mixture resembles very fine crumbs. Press mixture evenly into a greased 9 x 13-inch pan, using a piece of plastic wrap to press crumb mixture firmly in pan. Bake 17 to 20 minutes or until lightly browned.

Combine brown sugar, corn syrup, and ½ cup butter in a saucepan; bring to a boil over medium heat, stirring gently. Remove from heat. Stir one-fourth of hot mixture into beaten eggs; add to remaining hot mixture. Stir in pecans and vanilla. Pour filling over crust. Bake 34 to 35 minutes or until set. Cool completely in pan on a wire rack. Cut into bars.

Yield: about 16 large bars

Turtle Cookies

(pictured on page 100)

The title says it all. These are ooey-gooey-chocolaty treats anyone will be thrilled to receive. Give these cookies in the pan they were baked in or layer them on a tray.

> 2 cups all-purpose flour
> 1 cup firmly packed brown sugar
> ½ cup butter or margarine, softened
> 1 cup pecan halves
> ⅔ cup butter or margarine
> ½ cup firmly packed brown sugar
> 1 cup milk chocolate morsels

Preheat oven to 350 degrees. In a mixing bowl, combine flour, brown sugar, and butter; beat well. Pat mixture firmly into an ungreased 9 x 13-inch pan. Arrange pecans over crust.

Combine ⅔ cup butter and ½ cup brown sugar in a saucepan. Bring to a boil over medium heat, stirring constantly; cook 3 minutes, stirring constantly. Spoon mixture over pecans. Bake 18 to 20 minutes or until golden and bubbly.

Remove from oven; sprinkle top with chocolate morsels. Let stand 2 to 3 minutes or until slightly melted. Gently swirl chocolate with a knife, leaving some morsels whole. (Do not spread.) Cool, and cut into squares.

Yield: about 24 cookies

Morsels and Kisses and Chips—Oh, My!

Change the flavor of your cookie or candy simply by changing flavors of candy morsels, kisses, or chips.

- Morsels and chips now come in several flavors, making baking a new adventure. The flavors vary from traditional milk chocolate, semisweet chocolate, and cinnamon to peanut butter, butterscotch, white chips, mint chocolate, and raspberry.

- Change the taste and appearance of cookies that call for kisses by using white chocolate and milk chocolate swirled kisses instead of milk chocolate kisses.

- Add a little crunch to your cookies or candy by adding plain toffee bits, milk chocolate toffee bits, or almond toffee bits.

Lemon Butter Cookies

 **Big Batch**

(pictured on page 100)

It's easy to press out a lot of cookies in a wink using a cookie press—perfect when baking for gift giving.

>   2 cups butter, softened
>   1 cup confectioners sugar
>   3 cups all-purpose flour
>   1 teaspoon lemon extract
>   1 teaspoon grated lemon zest (optional)

Preheat oven to 325 degrees. Beat butter at medium speed of an electric mixer until creamy; gradually add confectioners sugar, beating well. Add flour, one cup at a time, beating well after each addition. Stir in lemon extract and, if desired, zest. Chill dough 30 minutes.

Form dough into desired shapes using a cookie press, and place on parchment paper-lined baking sheets. Bake 12 to 15 minutes per batch. Transfer to wire racks, and cool completely.

Yield: about 8 dozen cookies

Gingerbread Men

Make a few gingerbread boys to accompany the 5½-inch men by using a 3-inch cookie cutter.

>   2¼ cups sugar
>   ¾ cup water
>   ⅓ cup dark corn syrup
>   1½ tablespoons ground ginger
>   1¼ tablespoons ground cinnamon
>   2 teaspoons ground cloves
>   1¼ cups butter or margarine
>   1 tablespoon baking soda
>   1 tablespoon water
>   6 cups all-purpose flour
>   Decorations: sugar crystals, decorator
>   frosting, red cinnamon candies

In a saucepan, cook sugar, water, corn syrup, ginger, cinnamon, and cloves over medium heat, stirring until sugar dissolves. Add butter, stirring until melted.

Combine baking soda and 1 tablespoon water; stir into sugar mixture. Pour sugar mixture into a bowl; gradually add flour, beating at medium speed of a heavy-duty electric mixer until blended.

Preheat oven to 350 degrees. Divide dough into thirds. Roll one-third of dough to ⅛-inch thickness on a lightly floured surface. (Chill remaining dough.) Cut with a 5½-inch gingerbread man cutter, and place on lightly greased baking sheets.

Bake 10 to 12 minutes. Cool 1 minute on pan; remove cookies to wire racks, and cool completely. Repeat with remaining dough. Decorate as desired.

Yield: about 3 dozen cookies

Ornaments You Can Eat

Invited to a tree-trimming party? These no-bake cookie ornaments make a great gift to take along. Recipients can hang them on the tree, eat them, or both!

>   ¼ cup butter or margarine, softened
>   ⅓ cup light corn syrup
>   1 teaspoon vanilla extract
>   1 package (16 ounces) confectioners sugar,
>   sifted and divided
>   Green paste food coloring
>   Red cinnamon candies
>   Confectioners sugar
>   Tubes of decorator frosting
>   Assorted sprinkles

In a large mixing bowl, combine butter, syrup, and vanilla; beat at medium speed of an electric mixer until blended. Gradually add half of confectioners sugar, beating until smooth. Stir in enough remaining confectioners sugar to make a stiff dough, kneading with hands, if necessary.

Divide dough in half; wrap one portion in plastic wrap, and set aside. Knead green food coloring into remaining portion of dough.

To make wreaths, shape green dough into 18 (1-inch) balls. Roll each ball into a 5-inch rope, and connect ends of rope to form a circle. Decorate circles with red cinnamon candies to resemble wreaths.

To make cutout ornaments, roll out remaining portion of dough to about ¼-inch thickness on a surface lightly dusted with confectioners sugar. Cut into desired shapes, using 2-inch cookie cutters. Punch a hole in the top of each ornament, using a stir stick straw. Decorate ornaments with frosting and assorted sprinkles.

Lay wreaths and ornaments flat on waxed paper; set aside to partially dry (about 4 hours). Remove from waxed paper; transfer to wire racks. Dry 24 hours.

To hang, tie ornaments with ribbon.

Yield: about 3 dozen cookies

Marbled Cinnamon Hearts

Here's an art deco cookie as suitable for Valentine's Day as it is for Christmas. See it in our cookie box on page 185.

1 recipe Chocolate-Cinnamon Dough
1 recipe Vanilla Dough

Divide both doughs in half. Roll one portion of Chocolate-Cinnamon Dough into a 9-inch square on a lightly floured surface. Roll one portion of Vanilla Dough into a 9-inch square, and place on top of chocolate square. Continue rolling and stacking remaining two portions of dough, resulting in a 4-layer stack of alternating dough, pressing layers firmly to adhere.

Preheat oven to 350 degrees. Tear away a portion of stacked dough, and knead 2 or 3 times. (Too much kneading will prevent marbled look.) Roll dough to ⅛-inch thickness on a lightly floured surface. Cut with a 3-inch heart-shaped cookie cutter; place on ungreased baking sheets. Repeat procedure with remaining dough.

Bake 12 minutes or until lightly browned. Cool 1 minute on baking sheets; remove to wire racks, and cool completely.
Yield: about 6 dozen cookies

Chocolate-Cinnamon Dough

1 cup butter or margarine, softened
1 cup sugar
1 egg
1 teaspoon vanilla extract
2¼ cups all-purpose flour
1 teaspoon ground cinnamon
¾ teaspoon baking powder
¼ teaspoon salt
3 squares (1 ounce each) semisweet chocolate, melted

Beat butter and sugar at medium speed of an electric mixer until fluffy. Add egg and vanilla; beat until blended. Combine flour, cinnamon, baking powder, and salt; add to butter mixture, beating until blended. Add melted chocolate, beating until blended. Cover and chill dough 2 hours.

Vanilla Dough

½ cup butter or margarine, softened
½ cup vegetable shortening
1 cup sugar
1 egg
1½ teaspoons vanilla extract
2 cups all-purpose flour
¾ teaspoon baking powder
¼ teaspoon salt

Beat butter and shortening at medium speed of an electric mixer until creamy. Gradually add sugar, beating until light and fluffy. Add egg and vanilla; beat well. Combine flour, baking powder, and salt. Add to butter mixture; beat until blended. Cover and chill dough at least 2 hours.

Wheatmeal Shortbread

Pure ingredients blend to make a rich dough that bakes into tender-crisp shortbread cookies. Package them in a colorful bag accented with a beautiful bow.

1 cup butter, softened
¾ cup confectioners sugar
2 cups all-purpose flour
½ cup toasted wheat germ
2 to 3 tablespoons turbinado sugar or granulated sugar

Beat butter at medium speed of an electric mixer until creamy; gradually add confectioners sugar, beating well. Gradually add flour and wheat germ, beating just until blended. Turn dough out onto waxed paper. (Dough will be soft.) Pat dough into a rectangle; cover and chill 30 minutes or until firm.

Preheat oven to 325 degrees. Transfer dough to a lightly floured work surface; roll to ¼-inch thickness. Cut dough into 1 x 3-inch rectangles, using a fluted pastry wheel, or cut into squares with a fluted-edge square cookie cutter. Place 1 inch apart on ungreased baking sheets. Sprinkle with turbinado sugar.

Bake 19 to 20 minutes or until barely golden. Cool 5 minutes on baking sheets. Remove to wire racks, and cool completely.
Yield: about 3½ dozen cookies

Wheatmeal Shortbread

Cinnamon-Date Shortbread Sandwiches

Cinnamon-Date Shortbread Sandwiches

Sandwich a sweet date filling between these cinnamon cookies. Use your favorite holiday cookie cutters for variety and give as a gift in a decorative cookie jar.

Date Filling
½ cup butter or margarine, softened
⅓ cup granulated sugar
1 cup plus 2 tablespoons all-purpose flour
¾ teaspoon ground cinnamon
½ teaspoon vanilla extract
Confectioners sugar

Prepare Date Filling, and cool completely.

Preheat oven to 300 degrees. Beat butter at medium speed of an electric mixer until creamy; gradually add sugar, beating until light and fluffy. Add flour, cinnamon, and vanilla, mixing well. Shape dough into a ball. Roll dough to ⅛-inch thickness on a lightly floured surface; cut with 1½-inch or 2-inch round cutters. Use a ½-inch cutter to cut out a star in half of cookies. Pierce solid cookies with a fork or wooden pick.

Place cookies on ungreased baking sheets. Freeze 10 minutes. Bake 20 to 25 minutes or until cookies are very lightly browned. Cool 1 minute on baking sheets; remove to wire racks, and cool completely.

Spread each solid cookie with about ½ teaspoon of Date Filling. Top each cookie with a cutout cookie, pressing gently to adhere. Sprinkle with confectioners sugar.
Yield: about 2½ dozen cookies

Date Filling

½ (10-ounce) package chopped dates
1 tablespoon sugar
2½ tablespoons water
Pinch of salt

In a small saucepan, combine all ingredients; cook over medium heat, stirring constantly, 3 to 5 minutes or until thickened. Cool completely.
Yield: about ½ cup filling

Graham Stars

Whole grain, stone-ground flour gives these cookies a nutty aroma and taste. They're crisp and sturdy, ideal for making cookie garlands to take to a cookie swap.

- ½ cup butter, softened
- ½ cup firmly packed brown sugar
- ⅓ cup honey
- 1 egg
- 1 teaspoon vanilla extract
- 1½ cups all-purpose flour
- 1 cup whole-wheat graham flour
- ½ teaspoon baking soda
- ⅛ teaspoon salt
- ¾ cup confectioners sugar
- 1 teaspoon ground cinnamon

Beat butter at medium speed of an electric mixer until creamy; gradually add brown sugar and honey, beating well. Add egg and vanilla; beat well.

Combine flours, baking soda, and salt; gradually add to butter mixture, beating just until blended. Divide dough into four portions; shape each portion into a disc. Wrap in plastic wrap, and chill dough at least 1 hour.

Preheat oven to 375 degrees. Working with one portion of dough at a time, roll dough to ⅛-inch thickness on a lightly floured surface. Cut with a 3-inch star-shaped cookie cutter. Place cutouts on lightly greased baking sheets. Using a plastic drinking straw, make a hole in center of each star, and twist the straw to remove a tiny piece of dough (technique 1).

Bake 8 minutes or until edges of cookies are lightly browned. Cool slightly on baking sheets; remove to wire racks, and cool completely. Repeat procedure with remaining portions of dough.

Combine confectioners sugar and cinnamon in a large resealable plastic bag; seal and toss to combine. Add cookies to bag, about 5 at a time, and shake gently to coat. Remove coated cookies from bag, and repeat procedure with remaining cookies. String cookies onto raffia or ribbon, if desired (technique 2).

Yield: about 4 dozen cookies

Graham Stars

German Chocolate Slice 'n' Bakes

Toasted coconut and pecans give these cookies a yummy edge. You can make and freeze the dough up to a month ahead of time, and then slice and bake the cookies leisurely at gift-giving time.

    1½ cups flaked coconut
    1 cup butter, softened
    1½ cups sugar
    1 bar (4 ounces) sweet baking chocolate,
        melted and cooled
    1 egg
    1 teaspoon vanilla extract
    2½ cups all-purpose flour
    1 teaspoon baking powder
    ¼ teaspoon baking soda
    ⅛ teaspoon salt
    1½ cups finely chopped pecans, toasted
        Milk

Preheat oven to 350 degrees. Spread coconut in a shallow layer in a 10 x 15-inch jellyroll pan. Bake 13 to 14 minutes or until toasted and dry, stirring once. Cool and transfer coconut to a small resealable plastic bag. Finely crush coconut, and set aside.

Beat butter at medium speed of an electric mixer until creamy. Gradually add sugar, beating until light and fluffy. Add chocolate; beat well. Add egg and vanilla; beat well.

Combine flour, baking powder, baking soda, and salt; add to butter mixture, beating until blended. Stir in half of coconut.

Divide dough into thirds; place on 3 large sheets of plastic wrap. Roll each portion lengthwise in plastic wrap, and shape into a 10-inch log. Cover with plastic wrap, and chill logs 30 minutes. Reroll logs, if necessary.

Combine remaining coconut and pecans. Unwrap logs; brush lightly with milk, and roll in pecan-coconut mixture, pressing firmly to make coating adhere. Wrap in plastic wrap and freeze logs at least 8 hours or up to 1 month.

Preheat oven to 375 degrees. Cut into ¼-inch slices, using a sharp knife. Place 1 inch apart on ungreased baking sheets. Bake 8 to 9 minutes or until edges are browned. Cool 1 minute on baking sheets; remove to wire racks, and cool completely.
Yield: about 7 dozen cookies

Cranberry-Walnut Swirls

These unique slice-and-bake cookies roll cranberries and walnuts into the cookie dough jellyroll fashion. The swirl cookies burst with color and crunch.

    ½ cup butter or margarine, softened
    ¾ cup sugar
    1 egg
    1 teaspoon vanilla extract
    1½ cups all-purpose flour
    ¼ teaspoon baking powder
    ¼ teaspoon salt
    ⅓ cup finely chopped fresh cranberries
    ½ cup ground walnuts
    1 tablespoon grated orange zest

Beat butter and sugar at medium speed of an electric mixer until light and fluffy. Add egg and vanilla, beating until blended. Gradually add flour, baking powder, and salt, beating until blended. Cover and chill 1 hour.

Combine cranberries, walnuts, and orange zest.

Turn dough out onto a lightly floured surface, and roll into a 10-inch square. Sprinkle with cranberry mixture, leaving a ½-inch border on 2 opposite sides.

Roll up dough, jellyroll fashion, beginning at a bordered side. Cover and freeze at least 8 hours or up to 1 month.

Preheat oven to 375 degrees. Cut roll into ¼-inch-thick slices. Place slices on lightly greased baking sheets. Bake on top oven rack 14 to 15 minutes or until lightly browned. Remove to wire racks, and cool completely.
Yield: about 3 dozen cookies

Orange-Date-Nut Cookies

A great sturdy little cookie to mail—or to keep and serve with hot orange tea.

    1 package (10 ounces) chopped dates
    1 teaspoon grated orange zest
    1 tablespoon orange juice
    1 cup butter or margarine, softened
    1½ cups sugar
    1 egg
    1 teaspoon vanilla extract
    2½ cups all-purpose flour
    1½ teaspoons baking powder
    ½ teaspoon salt
    1 cup finely chopped toasted pecans, divided

Orange-Date-Nut Cookies

Line a 5 x 9-inch loaf pan with aluminum foil, allowing foil to extend over edges of pan. Set aside.

Position knife blade in food processor bowl; add first 3 ingredients. Process 45 seconds or until dates are finely chopped. Set aside.

Beat butter at medium speed of a heavy-duty electric mixer until blended. Gradually add sugar, beating until blended. Add egg and vanilla; beat well. Combine flour, baking powder, and salt; gradually add to butter mixture, beating at low speed just until blended.

Divide dough into three portions. Knead ½ cup pecans into one portion of dough; press into prepared pan. Knead date mixture into one portion of dough; press in pan over pecan mixture. Knead remaining ½ cup pecans into remaining portion of dough; press in pan over date mixture. Cover and chill at least 2 hours.

Preheat oven to 350 degrees. Invert loaf pan onto a cutting board, removing and discarding aluminum foil. Cut dough lengthwise into four sections. Cut each section of dough crosswise into ¼-inch slices. Place slices 1½ inches apart on lightly greased baking sheets.

Bake 9 to 10 minutes or until lightly browned. Cool slightly. Remove to wire racks, and cool completely.
Yield: about 8 dozen cookies

Eggnog Cookies

Brushing the cookie dough with an egg white mixture before baking helps to keep the sugar crystals in place. That's handy when packaging them up for giving.

- 1 cup butter or margarine, softened
- 2 cups sugar
- 5½ cups all-purpose flour
- 1 teaspoon baking soda
- ½ teaspoon ground nutmeg
- 1 cup eggnog
- 1 egg white, lightly beaten (optional)
- 1 tablespoon water (optional)
- Colored sugar crystals

Beat butter at medium speed of an electric mixer until creamy; gradually add 2 cups sugar, beating well.

Combine flour, baking soda, and nutmeg; add to butter mixture alternately with eggnog, beginning and ending with flour mixture. Cover and chill at least 1 hour.

Preheat oven to 375 degrees. Divide dough in half. Work with one portion of dough at a time, storing remainder in refrigerator. Roll each portion of dough to ⅛-inch thickness on a lightly floured surface. Cut with a 4-inch cookie cutter; place on lightly greased baking sheets.

Combine egg white and water in a small bowl; brush cookies with egg white mixture, if desired. Sprinkle with colored sugar. Bake 8 to 10 minutes or until lightly browned. Cool slightly on baking sheets; remove to wire racks, and cool completely.
Yield: about 4½ dozen cookies

Almond-Toffee Biscotti

Biscotti are designed for dunking in a cup of coffee, so they're a great partner for a pound of gourmet coffee.

- 2¾ cups all-purpose flour
- ½ cup granulated sugar
- ½ cup almond toffee bits
- ½ cup firmly packed brown sugar
- 2 teaspoons baking powder
- 1 tablespoon vegetable oil
- 1 teaspoon vanilla extract
- 3 eggs

Preheat oven to 350 degrees. In a large bowl, combine first 5 ingredients. Combine oil, vanilla, and eggs; add to flour mixture, stirring until well blended. (Dough will be dry and crumbly.) Turn dough out onto a lightly floured surface, and knead lightly 7 or 8 times. Divide dough in half. Shape each portion into an 8-inch-long roll. Place rolls 6 inches apart on a lightly greased baking sheet, and flatten each roll to 1-inch thickness.

Bake 35 minutes. Remove rolls from baking sheet; cool 10 minutes on a wire rack. Cut each roll diagonally into 15 (½-inch) slices. Place slices, cut sides down, on baking sheets. Reduce oven temperature to 325 degrees; bake 10 minutes. Turn cookies over; bake 10 more minutes. (Cookies will be slightly soft in center but will harden as they cool.) Remove to a wire rack, and cool completely.
Yield: about 2½ dozen biscotti

Raspberry-Fudge Truffles
(pictured on page 100)

A white chocolate coating cloaks these high-flavor truffles. A semisweet chocolate and raspberry filling hides inside—special enough for gift giving, for sure.

- 2 cups (12 ounces) semisweet chocolate morsels
- 2 packages (8 ounces each) cream cheese, softened
- 1 cup seedless raspberry preserves
- 2 tablespoons raspberry liqueur
- 3 cups vanilla wafer crumbs
- 10 squares (2 ounces each) chocolate candy coating
- 3 squares (1 ounce each) white chocolate

Microwave chocolate morsels in a 4-cup glass measuring cup on high power (100%) for 1½ to 2½ minutes or until melted, stirring every 30 seconds.

Beat cream cheese at medium speed of an electric mixer until smooth. Add melted chocolate, preserves, and liqueur, beating until blended. Stir in crumbs; cover and chill 4 hours.

Shape mixture into 1-inch balls; cover and freeze overnight.

Microwave chocolate coating in a 4-cup glass measuring cup on high power (100%) for 1½ to 2½ minutes or until melted, stirring every 30 seconds. Dip balls in coating using a sturdy wooden pick; place on waxed paper.

Place white chocolate in a small heavy-duty resealable plastic bag; seal. Submerge in hot water until chocolate melts; knead until smooth. Snip a tiny hole in one corner of bag, and drizzle mixture over truffles. Let stand until firm. Store in refrigerator or freeze up to 1 month, if desired.
Yield: about 8 dozen truffles

Chocolate-Bourbon Tartlets

Chocolate-Bourbon Tartlets

These crispy phyllo treats are extra tasty but also extra delicate because of the phyllo. Plan to package them in a single layer in a sturdy gift box.

36 frozen mini phyllo shells
⅓ cup semisweet chocolate mini-morsels
1 cup finely chopped pecans, toasted
¾ cup firmly packed light brown sugar
1 tablespoon butter or margarine, softened
¼ cup bourbon
1 egg, lightly beaten

Preheat oven to 350 degrees. Arrange shells on a lightly greased 10 x 15-inch jellyroll pan. Sprinkle chocolate mini-morsels into shells.

Stir together pecans, brown sugar, butter, bourbon, and egg. Spoon evenly into shells.

Bake 20 minutes or until golden brown. Remove to a wire rack, and cool completely. Store in an airtight container up to 3 days, or freeze up to 1 month.
Yield: about 3 dozen tartlets

Butterscotch-Peanut Fudge

Butterscotch-Peanut Fudge

Create an artistic gift with minimal effort by cutting this fudge in the shape of the gift box. A simple star and triangle cookie cutter work great to fill out the star-shaped box shown in the photo.

    1 package (11 ounces) butterscotch morsels
    1 can (14 ounces) sweetened condensed milk
    1½ cups miniature marshmallows
    ⅔ cup crunchy peanut butter
    1 teaspoon vanilla extract
    ⅛ teaspoon salt
    1 cup chopped dry-roasted peanuts

In a small heavy saucepan, cook butterscotch morsels, milk, and marshmallows over medium heat, stirring constantly, 5 to 6 minutes or until smooth; remove from heat.

Stir in crunchy peanut butter, vanilla, and salt until blended; stir in chopped peanuts. Pour into a buttered 9-inch square pan. Chill until firm; cut into squares. Store in refrigerator.
Yield: about 2½ pounds fudge

Pistachio Brittle

(pictured on page 116)

The soft shade of pistachios cooks up a green-speckled brittle almost too pretty to eat—we said almost.

    1½ cups firmly packed brown sugar
    3 tablespoons light corn syrup
    2 tablespoons water
    1½ tablespoons white vinegar
    ⅛ teaspoon salt
    ¼ cup plus 2 tablespoons butter, cut into pieces
    1¼ cups shelled pistachio nuts, toasted

In a heavy 2-quart nonstick saucepan, combine brown sugar and next 4 ingredients. Bring to a boil over medium-high heat, stirring constantly with a wooden spoon. Cover and cook over medium heat 2 to 3 minutes to wash down sugar crystals from sides of pan.

Uncover, and attach a candy thermometer to side of pan. Cook, stirring constantly, until thermometer registers 280 degrees. Add butter.

Cook, stirring constantly, until thermometer registers 300 degrees (hard crack stage). Remove thermometer. Quickly stir in pistachios, immediately pouring mixture onto a lightly greased jellyroll pan or large baking sheet. Quickly press nuts into a single layer within candy mixture. (Candy will not cover pan.) Cool completely; break brittle into pieces. Store in an airtight container.
Yield: about 1½ pounds brittle

Cinnamon Pralines

If you're using a lightweight saucepan, rely on a candy thermometer rather than a timer—these candies might cook more quickly than expected.

    1½ cups granulated sugar
    ¾ cup firmly packed light brown sugar
    ½ cup butter or margarine
    ½ cup milk
    1 teaspoon ground cinnamon
    1½ cups pecan halves

In a heavy 3-quart saucepan, cook all ingredients over low heat, stirring constantly, until sugars dissolve and butter melts. Bring mixture to a boil over medium heat; cook, stirring constantly, 3 minutes or until a candy thermometer registers 230 degrees.

Remove from heat, and beat with a wooden spoon 6 minutes or until mixture begins to thicken.

Working rapidly, drop by tablespoonfuls onto lightly greased waxed paper; let stand until firm.
Yield: about 2½ dozen pralines

Cherry Divinity

One recipe of this divinity will fill several mini tins for gift giving. Wash several shallow empty specialty coffee mix tins. Cover label with wide ribbon. Place divinity in paper candy cups, and stack in tin.

    3 cups sugar
    ¾ cup water
    ¾ cup light corn syrup
    ¼ teaspoon salt
    2 egg whites
    1 package (3 ounces) cherry-flavored gelatin
    1 cup chopped pecans or walnuts

In a large heavy saucepan, cook sugar, water, corn syrup, and salt over low heat, stirring constantly, until sugar dissolves.

Cover syrup mixture, and cook over medium heat 3 minutes. Uncover, cook over medium heat, without stirring, until mixture reaches hard ball stage or until a candy thermometer registers 258 degrees (about 18 minutes). Remove mixture from heat.

Beat egg whites at high speed of a heavy-duty mixer until foamy. Add gelatin, and beat until stiff peaks form.

Pour hot syrup in a thin stream over egg whites, beating constantly at high speed 4 minutes or until mixture holds its shape. Stir in pecans.

Drop mixture quickly by rounded teaspoonfuls onto waxed paper. Cool completely.
Yield: about 6 dozen candies

German Chocolate Cheesecake, page 152;
Spiced Apple Pie, page 133

Dazzling Desserts

This collection of luscious sweets is sure to impress your family and friends. Present the dessert on a keepsake platter or cake stand along with a handwritten note of holiday greetings.

Cranberry Streusel Pie

Cranberry Streusel Pie

Cranberry and walnuts add color and crunch to this pie that's perfect for spreading holiday cheer.

- ½ package (15 ounces) refrigerated pie crusts
- 2 cups fresh or frozen cranberries
- ¼ cup sugar
- ¼ cup firmly packed light brown sugar
- ¾ cup chopped walnuts
- ½ teaspoon ground cinnamon
- 1 egg
- ¼ cup butter or margarine, melted
- ⅓ cup sugar
- 3 tablespoons all-purpose flour

Preheat oven to 400 degrees. Fit pie crust into a 9-inch pie plate according to package directions; fold edges under, and crimp.

Stir together cranberries, sugars, walnuts, and cinnamon; spoon into pie crust.

Whisk together egg and remaining ingredients; pour over cranberry mixture.

Bake 20 minutes. Reduce oven temperature to 350 degrees, and bake 35 to 40 more minutes, shielding crust if necessary.
Yield: 1 (9-inch) pie

Spiced Apple Pie

(pictured on page 130)

This double-crust delight is brimming with juicy, sweetly tart apple slices infused with brewed tea, ginger, and cinnamon. The aromas will entice you as the pie bakes and the recipients as they savor each bite.

- 1 package (15 ounces) refrigerated pie crusts
- 1 cup sugar
- 2 tablespoons all-purpose flour
- ¼ teaspoon salt
- 1 teaspoon ground cinnamon
- ½ teaspoon ground ginger
- 3 tablespoons strongly brewed tea
- 1 tablespoon lemon juice
- 4 cups peeled, sliced Granny Smith apples (3 to 4 apples)
- 2 tablespoons butter or margarine, cut into pieces

Preheat oven to 450 degrees. Fit one pie crust into a 9-inch pie plate according to package directions.

Stir together sugar and next 6 ingredients. Alternate layers of apple and sugar mixture in pie crust, heaping apple slightly in center. Dot with butter.

Roll remaining pie crust to press out fold lines. Place pie crust over filling; trim off excess pastry along edges. Fold edges under, and crimp. Cut slits in top of pastry to allow steam to escape.

Bake 15 minutes. Reduce oven temperature to 350 degrees. Shield pie with aluminum foil to prevent excessive browning, and bake 50 more minutes. Cool pie completely on a wire rack.
Yield: 1 (9-inch) pie

Macadamia Pie

Use the extra pie crust to cut decorative shapes to adorn the pie edges for an extra-pretty pie that you'll enjoy sharing with friends.

- 1 package (15 ounces) refrigerated pie crusts
- 4 eggs, lightly beaten
- 1 cup light corn syrup
- ⅓ cup sugar
- 3 tablespoons butter or margarine, melted
- 1 vanilla bean, split lengthwise
- 2 jars (3½ ounces each) or 1 jar (7 ounces) macadamia nuts
- ½ cup flaked coconut

Preheat oven to 325 degrees. Fit one pie crust into a 9-inch pie plate according to package directions. Cut small circles or other desired shapes from remaining pie crust, using small cookie cutters. Arrange cutouts around edge of pie plate, pressing gently; set aside.

Combine eggs and next 3 ingredients in a medium bowl. Scrape vanilla bean seeds into egg mixture; discard vanilla bean pod. Stir mixture well. Stir in macadamia nuts and coconut. Pour filling into prepared pie crust.

Bake 40 to 45 minutes or until filling is set. Cool completely.
Yield: 1 (9-inch) pie

Orange-Pecan Pie — Make Ahead

Bake this orange-kissed pecan pie for holiday gift giving. The orange essence brings out the nutty flavor.

  3 eggs, lightly beaten
¾ cup sugar
  1 cup light corn syrup
  2 tablespoons grated orange zest
¼ cup fresh orange juice
  2 tablespoons butter or margarine, melted
  1 cup coarsely chopped pecans
  1 unbaked 9-inch pastry shell

Preheat oven to 325 degrees. In a large bowl, stir together first 6 ingredients. Arrange pecans in pastry shell; pour filling over pecans. Bake 50 minutes or until set. Cool on a wire rack.
Yield: 1 (9-inch) pie

Chocolate-Pecan Pie

Chocolate mini-morsels will convince kids who think they don't care for pecan pie that they really do!

¾ cup sugar
  6 tablespoons butter or margarine, melted
¾ cup light corn syrup
  3 eggs
  1 teaspoon vanilla extract
  1 cup coarsely chopped pecans
½ cup semisweet chocolate mini-morsels
  1 unbaked 9-inch pastry shell

Preheat oven to 350 degrees. In a large bowl, whisk together sugar and butter. Add corn syrup, eggs, and vanilla. Stir in pecans and chocolate mini-morsels; pour into pastry shell.
Bake 45 to 50 minutes or until set and lightly browned. Shield edges of pastry with aluminum foil during the last 10 minutes of baking to prevent excessive browning, if necessary. Cool on a wire rack.
Yield: 1 (9-inch) pie

Deep-Dish Pecan Pie

This is the grande dame of pecan pies. It slices best when chilled and served the next day, so it's perfect to make ahead for a friend. It's made in a springform pan, so transfer it to a giftable plate or a cardboard round for delivery.

  1 cup butter or margarine, softened
  2 packages (3 ounces each) cream cheese, softened
  2 cups all-purpose flour
¼ cup sugar
  1 bottle (16 ounces) light corn syrup
1½ cups firmly packed light brown sugar
⅓ cup butter or margarine, melted
  4 eggs, lightly beaten
  4 egg yolks, lightly beaten
  1 tablespoon vanilla extract
½ teaspoon salt
3½ cups pecan pieces or halves

Beat 1 cup butter and cream cheese at medium speed of an electric mixer until creamy. Gradually add flour and ¼ cup sugar, beating well. Shape dough into a flat disc; cover and chill 15 minutes. Roll chilled dough to a 13-inch circle; carefully transfer to an ungreased 9-inch springform pan. (We recommend covering the outside of your springform pan with aluminum foil before filling and baking this pie. It's a safeguard against leaks.) Press dough up sides of pan. Cover and chill.
Preheat oven to 375 degrees. Combine corn syrup, brown sugar, and melted butter in a large bowl; stir well with a wire whisk. Add eggs, egg yolks, vanilla, and salt; stir well. Stir in pecans. Pour filling into unbaked pastry-lined pan.
Bake 15 minutes. Reduce oven temperature to 300 degrees; bake 2 hours and 15 minutes, shielding pie with aluminum foil to prevent excess browning, if necessary. Cool completely on a wire rack. Cover and chill overnight. Carefully remove sides and bottom of springform pan, and transfer to a cardboard round or flat plate for gift giving.
Yield: 1 (9-inch) pie

Deep-Dish Pecan Pie

Fudge Pie

Package this pie along with Heavenly Fudge Sauce (page 152) for the ultimate gift for chocolate lovers.

> ¾ cup butter or margarine
> 3 squares (1 ounce each) unsweetened chocolate
> 3 eggs
> 1½ cups sugar
> ¾ cup all-purpose flour
> 1 teaspoon vanilla extract
> ½ cup chopped pecans, toasted

Preheat oven to 350 degrees. Cook butter and chocolate in a small saucepan over low heat, stirring often until melted.

Beat eggs at medium speed of an electric mixer 5 minutes. Gradually add sugar, beating until blended. Gradually add chocolate mixture, flour, and vanilla, beating until blended. Stir in ½ cup pecans.

Pour mixture into a lightly greased 9-inch pie plate.

Bake 35 to 40 minutes or until center is firm. Cool.

Yield: 1 (9-inch) pie

Pear Frangipan Tart

This showy French tart is superb served with vanilla bean ice cream. Frangipan refers to the buttery ground almond filling. Deliver it right in the tart pan along with the recipe so the recipient can recreate it at home.

> ½ cup butter, cut into pieces
> 1½ cups all-purpose flour
> ¼ teaspoon salt
> 3 tablespoons ice water
> 1¼ cups slivered almonds
> ½ cup sugar
> 2 tablespoons all-purpose flour
> ½ cup butter, softened
> 2 eggs
> 2 tablespoons confectioners sugar
> ¼ teaspoon salt
> 1 cup dry white wine
> 2 cups water
> 1 cup sugar
> 2 teaspoons vanilla extract
> 3 large Bosc pears, peeled
> 1 tablespoon butter or margarine, melted
> 1 tablespoon cornstarch

Pulse butter, flour, and salt in a food processor until mixture is crumbly. Slowly add ice water through food chute, pulsing until mixture forms a ball. Flatten dough to a 6-inch disc; wrap in plastic wrap and chill 1 hour.

Process almonds in food processor until finely ground. Combine almonds, ½ cup sugar, and 2 tablespoons flour in a small bowl; set aside.

Beat softened butter, eggs, confectioners sugar, and ¼ teaspoon salt at medium speed of an electric mixer until creamy. Combine almond and butter mixtures. Cover and chill 1 hour.

Preheat oven to 425 degrees. Roll pastry to ⅛-inch thickness on a floured surface. Fit pastry into a 10-inch tart pan; place on a baking sheet. Bake 12 minutes. Cool. Reduce oven temperature to 400 degrees.

Combine wine, 2 cups water, 1 cup sugar, and vanilla in a large saucepan; bring just to a boil. Add pears and simmer 8 minutes. Remove from heat. Cool pears completely in liquid. Remove pears and pat dry. Reserve 1 cup poaching liquid.

Cut pears in half vertically, remove cores, and cut pears into ¼-inch-thick lengthwise slices, keeping stem ends intact.

Spread almond mixture into baked tart shell. Arrange sliced pear halves over almond mixture, stem ends toward center. Fan pears slightly. Brush pears with melted butter. Bake 30 minutes or until golden.

Combine reserved 1 cup poaching liquid and cornstarch in a small saucepan, stirring until smooth. Cook over medium heat, stirring constantly, until mixture thickens. Boil 1 minute, stirring constantly. Remove from heat. Brush tart with glaze mixture. Remove sides of tart pan.

Yield: 1 (10-inch) tart

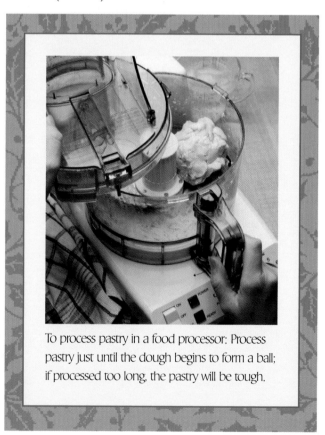

To process pastry in a food processor: Process pastry just until the dough begins to form a ball; if processed too long, the pastry will be tough.

Pear Frangipan Tart

Sugar Cookie Cran-Apple Cobbler

Sugar Cookie Cran-Apple Cobbler

You may never use regular pastry again when you sample this cookie dough cobbler crust. The cookie dough makes enough for two cobblers, so double the cobbler recipe to make two gifts or bake the extra dough into 2½ dozen cookies. To bake cookies, roll dough to ⅛-inch thickness and cut cookies using a 2½-inch cutter. Place cookies on an ungreased baking sheet and bake at 350 degrees for 8 minutes. Remove to wire racks to cool completely.

    2 cups fresh or frozen cranberries
 1½ cups sugar
    ⅔ cup water
    5 large cooking apples, peeled and chopped
    2 tablespoons cornstarch
    2 tablespoons water
    1 cup coarsely chopped pecans
    ½ cup raisins
    ½ recipe Brown Sugar Cookie Dough

In a Dutch oven or large saucepan, combine cranberries, sugar, water, and apples; bring to a boil. Cover, reduce heat, and simmer 10 minutes.

Combine cornstarch and 2 tablespoons water, stirring mixture until smooth. Add to cranberry mixture, stirring well. Bring to a boil; reduce heat, and simmer, uncovered, stirring constantly until thickened. Remove from heat; stir in pecans and raisins. Spoon mixture into a lightly greased 9 x 13-inch baking dish.

Flatten ½ of Brown Sugar Cookie Dough into a disc, and place between two sheets of waxed paper on a large cutting board. Roll dough into a 10-inch square.

Preheat oven to 350 degrees. Cut dough into 14 strips, using a pastry wheel or knife. Arrange strips diagonally in a lattice design over fruit mixture. Trim excess dough.

Bake, uncovered, 30 minutes or until filling is bubbly and cookie topping is done. Cool cobbler 10 minutes on a wire rack.
Yield: about 8 servings

Brown Sugar Cookie Dough

    1 cup butter, softened
 1½ cups firmly packed dark brown sugar
    1 egg
    1 teaspoon vanilla extract
    3 cups all-purpose flour
    1 teaspoon baking soda
    ½ teaspoon salt

Beat butter at medium speed of an electric mixer until creamy. Gradually add brown sugar, beating well.

Add egg and vanilla, beating well.

Combine flour, baking soda, and salt; add to butter mixture, beating just until blended.

Use dough as directed to top the cobbler.
Yield: dough for 2 cobblers

Directions for gift card: Reheat cobbler at 350 degrees for 25 minutes. Serve warm. Top with vanilla ice cream, if desired.

Ready-to-Bake Apple Crisp

Deliver this homestyle dessert oven-ready so friends can pop it in their oven and enjoy it hot.

    3 Granny Smith apples, peeled and sliced
    2 cups fresh cranberries
    1 can (8 ounces) crushed pineapple in juice, undrained
    ½ cup sugar
    1 cup firmly packed brown sugar
    ¼ cup all-purpose flour
    ½ cup butter or margarine
    1 cup uncooked regular oats
    1 cup chopped pecans

Preheat oven to 375 degrees. Layer apples, cranberries, and pineapple in a lightly greased 9 x 13-inch baking dish; sprinkle with ½ cup sugar.

Combine brown sugar and flour; with a pastry blender, cut in butter until mixture is crumbly. Stir in oats and pecans. Sprinkle oat mixture evenly over fruit mixture; cover and chill.
Yield: about 8 servings

Directions for gift card: Chill up to 24 hours before baking. When ready to bake, let stand at room temperature 30 minutes. Preheat oven to 375 degrees. Bake, uncovered, 30 minutes or until bubbly and thoroughly heated. Serve with whipped cream or ice cream.

Graham Cracker-Nut Crumble

Graham Cracker-Nut Crumble

This torte will stick to the pie plate and doesn't slice like a pie. Just spoon it onto serving plates like a cobbler.

> 3 eggs, separated
> 1 cup graham cracker crumbs
> 1 cup firmly packed brown sugar
> 1 teaspoon baking powder
> ¼ teaspoon salt
> ½ teaspoon vanilla extract
> ½ cup chopped pecans

Preheat oven to 350 degrees. Combine egg yolks and next 6 ingredients, stirring well.

Beat egg whites at high speed of an electric mixer until stiff peaks form; fold into crumb mixture. Spoon into a greased and floured 9-inch pie plate.

Bake 30 minutes.

Yield: 1 (9-inch) dessert

Directions for gift card: Serve chilled, or reheat if desired. To reheat, microwave on medium power (50%) for 3 minutes, turning once. To serve, spoon mixture onto serving plates like a cobbler; serve with whipped cream, if desired.

Cinnamon-Raisin Bread Pudding

Thick slices of raisin bread are doused with a sweetly spiced custard to create this breakfast indulgence. Presliced bread won't be thick enough to soak up all the custard, so be sure to buy an unsliced loaf.

> 1 unsliced loaf (¾ pound) cinnamon-raisin bread
> 5 eggs
> 3 egg yolks
> 1 cup half and half
> ¾ cup milk
> 1 tablespoon vanilla extract
> 1 teaspoon ground cinnamon
> ½ teaspoon ground nutmeg
> ½ cup butter or margarine, melted

Trim crust from bread; cut into 4 (2-inch-thick) slices. Arrange slices in a well-greased 9-inch square pan.

Whisk together eggs and next 6 ingredients in a large bowl. Spoon egg mixture over bread slices. Drizzle melted butter over egg mixture. Cover and chill.

Yield: about 4 to 6 servings

Directions for gift card: Keep refrigerated until ready to bake, up to 24 hours. Preheat oven to 350 degrees. Bake, uncovered, 55 to 60 minutes or until set. Sprinkle with confectioners sugar. Serve warm.

Bread Pudding with Whiskey Sauce

We think you'll agree this is one of the best bread puddings around—so good that it received our highest rating.

> 1 loaf (1 pound) dry French bread
> 4 cups milk
> 4 eggs, beaten
> 2 cups sugar
> 2 tablespoons vanilla extract
> 1 cup raisins
> 2 apples, peeled, cored, and cubed
> 1 can (8 ounces) crushed pineapple, drained
> ¼ cup butter, melted
> Whiskey Sauce

Preheat oven to 350 degrees. Tear bread into small pieces; place in a large bowl. Add milk to bowl; let mixture stand 10 minutes. Stir mixture well with a wooden spoon. Add eggs, sugar, and vanilla; stir well. Stir in raisins, apple, and pineapple. Pour butter into a 9 x 13-inch pan; tilt pan to coat evenly. Spoon pudding mixture into pan. Bake, uncovered, 55 to 60 minutes. Remove from oven, and cool slightly.

Yield: about 16 servings

Note: To dry out fresh bread, tear bread into small pieces; bake at 200 degrees for 1 hour, turning once.

Directions for gift card: Reheat, uncovered, at 350 degrees for 30 minutes. Serve warm with Whiskey Sauce.

Whiskey Sauce

> ½ cup melted butter
> 1 cup sugar
> ⅓ cup bourbon, divided
> 1 egg, beaten

In a heavy saucepan, combine butter and sugar; cook over medium heat until butter melts. Add ½ of bourbon, and simmer 3 minutes; stirring well. Reduce heat to medium-low.

Beat egg until thick and pale. Gradually stir about ¼ of hot mixture into egg mixture; add to remaining hot mixture, stirring constantly. Stir in remaining bourbon.

Yield: about 1⅓ cups sauce

Directions for gift card: Reheat on medium power (50%) for 2 minutes, stirring after 1 minute.

Bourbon-Chocolate Torte

Pair this rich chocolate cake with Heavenly Fudge Sauce (page 152) for the chocoholics on your list.

     2 packages (8 ounces each) semisweet
         chocolate squares, chopped
     1 cup butter, cut into pieces
     2 cups sugar
     ¾ cup pecan pieces, toasted
     ¼ cup bourbon
     8 eggs
     1 tablespoon confectioners sugar

Grease a 10-inch springform pan, and line bottom with parchment paper or waxed paper. Grease paper. Set aside.

Microwave chocolate and butter in a 1-quart glass measuring cup on medium power (50%) for 5 to 7 minutes or until melted, stirring after each minute. Let stand 15 minutes.

Preheat oven to 350 degrees. Process 2 cups sugar and pecans in a food processor until ground, stopping once to scrape down sides. Transfer to a large mixing bowl.

Stir bourbon into nut mixture. Add eggs, 1 at a time, beating at low speed of an electric mixer until blended after each addition.

Add chocolate mixture, and beat at low speed until blended. Pour into prepared pan.

Bake 30 minutes or until set. Cool completely in pan on a wire rack. Remove sides of pan. Cover torte, and chill 8 hours. Transfer to a giftable plate or cardboard round. Sprinkle with confectioners sugar.
Yield: 1 (10-inch) torte

Directions for gift card: Serve with Heavenly Fudge Sauce. Reheat refrigerated sauce in the microwave on medium power (50%) for 2 minutes, stirring once.

Vanilla Bean Loaf Cake

It's the tiny seeds inside the bean that tell of vanilla's essence. Use the seeds to make vanilla sugar in this simple buttery cake, which also absorbs a vanilla glaze.

     1¼ cups sugar
      1 vanilla bean
      2 cups plus 2 tablespoons sifted
          cake flour
      1 teaspoon baking powder
      ½ teaspoon salt
      1 cup unsalted butter, softened
      4 eggs
      ⅓ cup confectioners sugar
      1 tablespoon milk
      1 teaspoon vanilla extract

Pour 1¼ cups sugar into a jar. Split vanilla bean in half lengthwise. Scrape tiny vanilla bean seeds into sugar; cut bean into 1-inch pieces, and add to vanilla sugar. Cover and shake vigorously to mix, or stir well. Let stand 24 hours.

Preheat oven to 325 degrees. Combine flour, baking powder, and salt; stir well. Beat butter at low speed of an electric mixer until creamy. Remove and discard pieces of vanilla bean from sugar. Gradually add vanilla sugar to butter, beating at medium speed until light and fluffy. Add eggs, 1 at a time, beating well after each addition. Gradually add flour mixture to butter mixture, beating at low speed just until blended.

Pour batter into a lightly greased and floured 5 x 9-inch loaf pan. Bake 1 hour or until a wooden pick inserted in center of cake comes out clean. Cool in pan on a wire rack 15 minutes.

Combine confectioners sugar, milk, and vanilla; stir well. Prick tiny holes in top of loaf with a wooden pick. Spoon glaze mixture over warm loaf; cool in pan on wire rack 15 more minutes. Remove from pan, and cool completely on wire rack.
Yield: 1 loaf

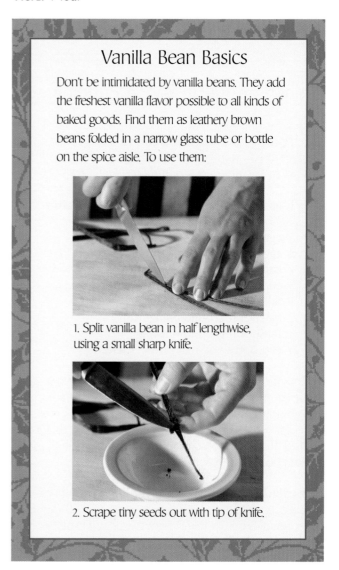

Vanilla Bean Basics

Don't be intimidated by vanilla beans. They add the freshest vanilla flavor possible to all kinds of baked goods. Find them as leathery brown beans folded in a narrow glass tube or bottle on the spice aisle. To use them:

1. Split vanilla bean in half lengthwise, using a small sharp knife.

2. Scrape tiny seeds out with tip of knife.

Vanilla Bean Loaf Cake

Mexican Mocha Angel Food Cake

This may be the easiest homemade cake possible . . . perfect for pairing alongside a jar of the Mexican Mocha Spice Mix so the recipient can enjoy it over and over.

1 package (14½ ounces) angel food cake mix
¼ cup Mexican Mocha Spice Mix, divided (page 27)

Prepare cake batter according to package directions. Spoon ⅓ of batter into an ungreased 10-inch tube pan. Sprinkle with 2 tablespoons Mexican Mocha Spice Mix. Repeat layers; top with remaining ⅓ of batter. Gently swirl batter with a knife. Bake according to package directions.
Yield: 1 (10-inch) cake

Brown Sugar-Rum Pound Cakes

This old-fashioned recipe yields two loaf cakes or small Bundt cakes. Pour the Hot Rum Glaze over the top of each as soon as you remove them from the pan so the glaze can firm up as the cakes cool.

½ cup chopped pecans
1¼ cups butter, softened
1 package (16 ounces) light brown sugar
¼ cup sugar
4 eggs
⅔ cup milk
¼ cup dark rum
2 teaspoons vanilla extract
2½ cups all-purpose flour
¾ teaspoon baking powder
¼ teaspoon salt
Hot Rum Glaze

Preheat oven to 325 degrees. Grease and flour 2 (6-cup) Bundt pans or 2 (5 x 9-inch) loaf pans, and sprinkle each evenly with pecans.

Beat butter at medium speed of an electric mixer about 2 minutes or until creamy. Gradually add sugars, beating 5 to 7 minutes. Add eggs, 1 at a time, beating just until yellow disappears.

Combine milk, rum, and vanilla.

Combine flour, baking powder, and salt; add to butter mixture alternately with milk mixture, beginning and ending with flour mixture. Beat at low speed just until blended after each addition. Pour evenly into prepared pans.

Bake 50 to 55 minutes or until a wooden pick inserted in center of cake comes out clean. Cool in pans on wire racks 10 to 15 minutes; remove from pans, and drizzle with glaze. Cool completely on wire racks.
Yield: 2 (8-inch) cakes

Hot Rum Glaze

½ cup sugar
¼ cup butter
2 tablespoons light rum
2 tablespoons water

Bring all ingredients to a boil in a saucepan; boil, stirring occasionally, 3 minutes.
Yield: about 1 cup glaze

Directions for gift card: Serve with sweetened whipped cream, if desired.

Pear Preserves Cake

Here's a homestyle spice cake friends will enjoy warm and toasted for breakfast or at room temperature for snacking all day long.

1 cup vegetable shortening
2½ cups sugar
4 eggs
1 teaspoon vanilla extract
3¼ cups all-purpose flour
¾ teaspoon baking soda
1 teaspoon ground cinnamon
1 teaspoon ground cloves
1 teaspoon ground allspice
1 cup buttermilk
1 jar (11.5 ounces) pear preserves
1 cup chopped pecans
Confectioners sugar

Preheat oven to 325 degrees. Beat shortening and sugar at medium speed of an electric mixer until fluffy. Add eggs, beating well. Stir in vanilla.

Combine flour and next 4 ingredients; add to shortening mixture alternately with buttermilk, beginning and ending with flour mixture. Beat at low speed just until blended after each addition.

Fold in pear preserves and pecans. Pour into a greased and floured 10-inch tube pan.

Bake 1 hour and 20 minutes or until a long wooden pick inserted in center of cake comes out clean. Cool in pan on a wire rack 15 minutes; remove from pan, and cool completely on wire rack. Dust top of cake with confectioners sugar.
Yield: 1 (10-inch) cake

Pear Preserves Cake

Fresh Ginger Pound Cake with Glazed Cranberry Ambrosia

Fresh Ginger Pound Cake with Glazed Cranberry Ambrosia

Fresh Ginger Pound Cake with Glazed Cranberry Ambrosia is a luscious gift combination, but either is welcome on its own. You can even serve the ambrosia over ice cream.

> ⅔ cup butter or margarine, softened
> 1 cup sugar
> 3 eggs
> 2¼ cups all-purpose flour
> 1 teaspoon baking powder
> 1 teaspoon salt
> ½ cup milk
> 2 tablespoons minced fresh ginger
> ½ teaspoon vanilla extract
> Glazed Cranberry Ambrosia

Preheat oven to 325 degrees. Beat butter at medium speed of an electric mixer 2 minutes or until creamy; gradually add sugar, and beat 5 to 7 minutes. Add eggs, 1 at a time, beating just until yellow disappears.

Combine flour, baking powder, and salt; add to butter mixture alternately with milk, beginning and ending with flour mixture. Beat at low speed just until blended after each addition. Stir in ginger and vanilla. Pour batter into a greased and floured 5 × 9-inch loaf pan.

Bake 1 hour and 20 minutes or until a long wooden pick inserted in center of cake comes out clean. Cool in pan on a wire rack 10 minutes; remove from pan, and cool completely on wire rack.
Yield: 1 (9-inch) loaf

Directions for gift card: Serve with Glazed Cranberry Ambrosia.

Glazed Cranberry Ambrosia

> 1 cup fresh or frozen cranberries, thawed
> ¼ cup sugar
> 2 tablespoons water
> 1 tablespoon minced fresh ginger
> 1 tablespoon grated orange zest
> 5 oranges, peeled and sectioned

In a small saucepan, combine first 4 ingredients; cover and cook over medium heat 2 minutes. Uncover and cook, stirring constantly, 3 minutes or until cranberry skins pop. Remove from heat, and stir in orange zest. Cool 15 minutes.

Stir in orange sections, and chill 8 hours.
Yield: about 2½ cups ambrosia

Holiday Brownie Cupcakes

Here's a gift kids love that's easy enough for them to make, too. So be sure to share the recipe.

> 1 package (21 ounces) brownie mix
> ½ cup vegetable oil
> ¼ cup cranberry juice
> 2 eggs
> Toppings: semisweet chocolate morsels, candy-coated chocolate pieces, chopped pecans, holiday candy sprinkles
> Confectioners sugar (optional)

Preheat oven to 350 degrees. Stir together first 4 ingredients until smooth. Spoon batter into 12 lightly greased muffin cups. Sprinkle with desired toppings.

Bake 20 minutes or until a wooden pick inserted in center of cupcakes comes out clean. Remove from pan, and cool on a wire rack. If desired, sprinkle with confectioners sugar.
Yield: about 12 servings

Apple-Oat Snack Squares

Deliver this old-fashioned spice cake in a disposable baking pan or cut it into squares and transfer them to a plate. Either way, your friends will relish them with a glass of milk right away!

> 3 cups all-purpose baking mix
> 2 cups uncooked quick-cooking oats
> ⅔ cup firmly packed light brown sugar
> 1 teaspoon ground cinnamon
> ½ cup butter or margarine, cut into pieces
> 1 cup milk
> 1 can (21 ounces) apple fruit filling
> 2 tablespoons light brown sugar

Preheat oven to 350 degrees. In a medium bowl, stir together baking mix, oats, ⅔ cup brown sugar, and cinnamon; with a pastry blender, cut in butter until crumbly. Stir in milk just until dry ingredients are moistened. Fold in fruit filling, and spoon into a lightly greased 9 × 13-inch pan. Sprinkle with 2 tablespoons brown sugar.

Bake 40 minutes or until golden. Cool on a wire rack, and cut into squares.
Yield: about 16 squares

White Chocolate Chunk Fruitcake

The wooden pick test won't accurately indicate when this cake is done. Use your fruitcake intuition—the cake is baked when it rises to stand firm in the pan and has a golden crust on top. Cool it in the pan 30 minutes; then cool completely on a wire rack before wrapping it up.

- ¼ cup butter, softened
- ½ cup firmly packed brown sugar
- 3 eggs
- 1⅓ cups all-purpose flour
- 2 teaspoons baking powder
- ¼ teaspoon salt
- 8 ounces white chocolate, chopped
- 1 cup cashews, coarsely chopped
- ¾ cup flaked coconut
- ⅓ cup candied diced orange peel
- 1 package (3 ounces) dried cranberries

Preheat oven to 300 degrees. Grease a 5 x 9-inch loaf pan; line with waxed paper. Grease and flour waxed paper. Set aside.

Beat butter at medium speed of an electric mixer until creamy; gradually add brown sugar, beating well. Add eggs, 1 at a time, beating after each addition.

Combine flour, baking powder, and salt; add to butter mixture, beating at low speed until blended. Fold in white chocolate and remaining ingredients. (Batter will be very chunky and thick.)

Spoon batter into prepared pan. Bake 1 hour and 15 minutes. Run a sharp knife around edge of pan to loosen fruitcake; cool in pan on a wire rack 30 minutes. Remove cake from pan; peel off waxed paper. Cool completely on wire rack.

Yield: 1 (5 x 9-inch) cake

A Splash of Liqueur

Spice up your fruitcake with flavored liqueurs for a twist on the traditional fruitcake. Make it a culinary delight by adding Amaretto, Godiva, Kahlúa, or any fruit-flavored liqueur to embellish the flavor or accent certain ingredients in your favorite fruitcake.

Add a tablespoon or two of the desired liqueur to the mix of ingredients before baking. And brush more liqueur over the top of your fruitcake after baking. The liqueur will penetrate the cake to give it that final flavor touch.

Little Chocolate-Kahlúa Fruitcakes

This fruitcake recipe is like none other. It's gooey and brownielike and unforgettable. You can make these little cakes up to a month ahead of time and splash them weekly with Kahlúa for extra punch.

- 1 cup butter
- 6 squares (1 ounce each) semisweet chocolate
- 1 teaspoon instant coffee granules
- 1 cup firmly packed brown sugar
- 3 eggs, separated
- 6 tablespoons Kahlúa or other coffee-flavored liqueur, divided
- 1 teaspoon vanilla extract
- 2 cups all-purpose flour, divided
- ½ teaspoon baking soda
- ¼ teaspoon salt
- 1 container (10 ounces) whole pitted dates, chopped (about 1¾ cups)
- 1½ cups chopped pecans, toasted
- 1 cup semisweet chocolate mega-morsels or regular morsels
- ¾ cup dried apricots, chopped
- Additional Kahlúa

Preheat oven to 300 degrees. Grease 5 (3 x 6-inch) loaf pans. Line bottoms of loaf pans with waxed paper; set aside.

Melt butter and chocolate in a heavy saucepan over low heat, stirring often. Stir in coffee granules. Remove mixture from heat, and cool 15 minutes. Pour into a large bowl. Stir in brown sugar. Add egg yolks, stirring well. Add 2 tablespoons Kahlúa and vanilla; stir well.

Combine 1½ cups flour, baking soda, and salt; add to chocolate mixture. Combine dates and next 3 ingredients; sprinkle with remaining ½ cup flour, tossing to coat. Stir fruit mixture into batter. Beat egg whites at high speed of an electric mixer until stiff peaks form; fold into batter.

Spoon batter evenly into prepared pans. Bake 1 hour and 15 minutes or until a wooden pick inserted in center of cake comes out clean. Cool in pans on a wire rack 10 minutes; remove from pans, and brush loaves with remaining ¼ cup Kahlúa. Cool completely on wire rack.

Wrap fruitcakes in Kahlúa-soaked cheesecloth. Store in an airtight container in a cool place at least 1 week before serving. Pour a small amount of Kahlúa over each loaf every week up to 1 month.

Yield: 5 loaves

Little Chocolate-Kahlúa Fruitcakes

Spiced Nut Fruitcake

Here's a cake you can make a week or so ahead to leave time for soaking it in sherry-wrapped cheesecloth. It just gets better and better over time.

  2 cups golden raisins
  ¾ cup dry sherry
  2 cups chopped candied pineapple (about 1 pound)
  1½ cups chopped red candied cherries (about ¾ pound)
  1½ cups chopped green candied cherries (about ¾ pound)
  4 cups chopped pecans
  3 cups all-purpose flour, divided
  ¾ cup butter or margarine, softened
  ¾ cup sugar
  ¾ cup firmly packed brown sugar
  6 eggs
  ¼ teaspoon salt

  1 teaspoon ground allspice
  1 teaspoon ground cinnamon
  ¾ teaspoon ground mace (optional)
  ¾ cup whipping cream
  1 jar (10 ounces) strawberry preserves
  ¾ teaspoon almond extract
  ¾ teaspoon orange extract
  ¾ teaspoon vanilla extract

Soak raisins in sherry 8 hours; drain and set aside.

Preheat oven to 275 degrees. Combine pineapple, candied cherries, pecans, and 1 cup flour, tossing to coat. Set aside.

Beat butter at medium speed of an electric mixer until fluffy; gradually add sugars, beating well. Add eggs, 1 at a time, beating well after each addition.

Combine remaining 2 cups flour, salt, allspice, cinnamon, and, if desired, mace. Add to butter mixture alternately with whipping cream, beginning and ending with flour mixture. Beat at low speed just until blended after each addition. Add preserves and extracts,

Spiced Nut Fruitcake

beating well. Stir in reserved raisins and fruit mixture. Spoon into a greased and floured 10-inch tube pan.

Bake 3 hours or until a long wooden pick inserted in center of cake comes out clean. Cool in pan on a wire rack 20 minutes; remove from pan, and cool completely on wire rack. If desired, soak cheesecloth in 2/3 cup dry sherry, wrap around cake, and place in an airtight container; refrigerate 7 to 10 days.
Yield: 1 (10-inch) cake

White Fruitcake Make Ahead

For the fruitcake lovers on your list, here's a classic recipe that tastes great whether or not you choose to soak it in brandy.

    1 cup butter or margarine, softened
    1 cup sugar
    2 eggs
    1 teaspoon orange extract
    1 teaspoon lemon extract
    3 cups cake flour, divided
    2 teaspoons baking powder
    1/2 teaspoon baking soda
    1/2 teaspoon salt
    1/2 cup peach nectar
    1 cup flaked coconut
    1 cup chopped candied pineapple (about 1/2 pound)
    1 cup chopped candied cherries (about 1/2 pound)
    1 cup golden raisins (about 1/2 pound)
    1 cup chopped crystallized ginger
    2 cups chopped pecans, toasted
    6 egg whites
      Peach brandy (optional)

Preheat oven to 275 degrees. Beat butter and sugar at medium speed of an electric mixer until fluffy. Add eggs, 1 at a time, beating well after each addition. Stir in extracts.

Combine 2 cups cake flour and next 3 ingredients; add to butter mixture alternately with nectar, beginning and ending with flour mixture. Beat at low speed just until blended after each addition.

Stir together remaining 1 cup cake flour, coconut, and next 4 ingredients. Stir fruit mixture and pecans into batter.

Beat egg whites at high speed until stiff peaks form. Fold into batter. Pour into a greased and floured 10-inch tube pan.

Bake 2 hours or until a long wooden pick inserted in center of cake comes out clean. Cool on a wire rack. If desired, wrap in cheesecloth, and soak with 1 cup peach brandy for two weeks.
Yield: 1 (10-inch) cake

Candy Bar Cheesecake

Your favorite milk chocolate candy bar is melted and folded into the cheesecake mixture. You can crumble an extra candy bar on top along with the nuts if you'd like to hint at the flavor.

    3/4 cup graham cracker crumbs
    2/3 cup finely chopped walnuts
    2 tablespoons sugar
    2 tablespoons butter or margarine, melted
    4 packages (3 ounces each) cream cheese, softened
    3/4 cup sugar
    2 tablespoons cocoa
      Dash of salt
    2 eggs
    1 milk chocolate candy bar (8 ounces), melted
    1/2 cup sour cream
    1/2 teaspoon vanilla extract
      Sour Cream Topping
      Chopped walnuts

Preheat oven to 325 degrees. Combine first 4 ingredients; firmly press mixture on bottom and 2 inches up sides of an 8-inch springform pan.

Beat cream cheese at medium speed of an electric mixer until fluffy. Combine 3/4 cup sugar, cocoa, and salt; gradually add to cream cheese, beating well. Add eggs, 1 at a time, beating after each addition. Stir in melted chocolate, sour cream, and vanilla, blending well.

Pour into prepared pan. Bake 40 minutes. Turn off oven, and leave cheesecake in closed oven 30 minutes. Remove from oven, and cool on a wire rack; chill. Remove sides of springform pan; spread with Sour Cream Topping, and sprinkle with walnuts. Store in refrigerator.
Yield: 1 (8-inch) cheesecake

Sour Cream Topping

    1/2 cup sour cream
    2 tablespoons sugar
    1/2 teaspoon vanilla extract

Combine all ingredients.
Yield: about 1/2 cup topping

German Chocolate Cheesecake

(pictured on page 130)

The popular cake takes a creamy turn in this boldly chocolate cheesecake.

 1½ cups chocolate wafer cookie crumbs (about 30 cookies)
 3 tablespoons sugar
 ¼ cup butter, melted
 4 packages (8 ounces each) cream cheese, softened
 3 eggs
 1 cup sugar
 1 package (7 ounces) flaked coconut
 1 package (11.5 ounces) milk chocolate morsels
 ½ cup chopped pecans, toasted
 1 teaspoon vanilla extract
 ½ cup (3 ounces) milk chocolate morsels
   Toasted flaked coconut to garnish

Preheat oven to 350 degrees. Stir together cookie crumbs, 3 tablespoons sugar, and butter; press mixture into bottom of a 10-inch springform pan. Bake 8 minutes. Cool.

Beat cream cheese, eggs, and 1 cup sugar at medium speed of an electric mixer until fluffy. Stir in coconut and next 3 ingredients. Pour into prepared pan.

Bake 1 hour or until cheesecake is almost set in center. Cool on a wire rack. Cover; chill 8 hours.

Place ½ cup milk chocolate morsels in a resealable plastic bag; seal. Submerge bag in warm water until morsels melt. Snip a tiny hole in one corner of bag; drizzle chocolate over cheesecake.

Garnish with toasted coconut. Store in refrigerator.
Yield: 1 (10-inch) cheesecake

Heavenly Fudge Sauce

Spoon this heavenly sauce into an attractive jar. It makes a nice gift alone or paired with another gift, such as Bourbon-Chocolate Torte (page 142) or Fudge Pie (page 136).

 1 package (12 ounces) semisweet chocolate morsels
 1 tablespoon butter or margarine
 ½ cup whipping cream
 ¼ cup strongly brewed coffee

Place chocolate morsels and butter in a heavy saucepan. Cook over low heat until chocolate and butter melt, stirring often. Gradually whisk in whipping cream. Cook, stirring constantly, 2 to 3 minutes or until smooth. Remove from heat; stir in coffee. Cool. Cover and chill.
Yield: about 1¾ cups sauce

Almond Cheesecake

This showstopping Almond Cheesecake is a favorite of our staff. If your cheesecake cracks when it's baked, don't worry. The sour cream topping hides any flaws, so it's pretty enough to give every time.

 40 vanilla wafers
 ¾ cup slivered almonds, toasted
 ⅓ cup sugar
 ⅓ cup butter or margarine, melted
 3 packages (8 ounces each) cream cheese, softened
 1 cup sugar
 4 eggs
 ⅓ cup whipping cream
 ¼ cup almond-flavored liqueur
 2 teaspoons vanilla extract, divided
 2 cartons (8 ounces each) sour cream
 1 tablespoon sugar
 1 tablespoon almond-flavored liqueur
   Sliced almonds, sliced fresh strawberries, and kiwifruit slices to garnish

Preheat oven to 350 degrees. Position knife blade in food processor bowl; add first 3 ingredients. Process until crushed. Add butter, and process until blended.

Press mixture into bottom and 1¾ inches up sides of a lightly greased 9-inch springform pan; set aside.

Combine cream cheese and 1 cup sugar; beat at high speed of an electric mixer until light and fluffy. Add eggs, 1 at a time, beating well after each addition. Add whipping cream, ¼ cup almond-flavored liqueur, and 1 teaspoon vanilla, beating well at medium speed. Pour into prepared crust.

Bake 30 minutes. Reduce heat to 225 degrees, and bake 1 hour. Cool cheesecake in pan on a wire rack 5 minutes.

Combine remaining 1 teaspoon vanilla, sour cream, 1 tablespoon sugar, and 1 tablespoon liqueur; spread evenly over warm cheesecake. Return to oven, and bake 5 more minutes.

Cool in pan on wire rack 30 minutes. Gently run a knife around edge of pan to release sides; cool completely in pan on wire rack. Cover and chill 8 hours.

Remove sides of pan; garnish with almonds, strawberries, and kiwifruit.
Yield: 1 (9-inch) cheesecake

Almond Cheesecake

Chocolate Chip "Sandwich" Squares, page 159;
Santa's Boot Cookies, page 163;
Christmas Popcorn, page 159

Elfin Delights

Children love holiday snacks, so be sure to include them in the fun by making some of these playful treats. Great gift ideas and kid-friendly foods make this collection ideal for shaping holiday traditions.

Reindeer Fodder Mix

Reindeer Fodder Mix

Fill decorated take-out boxes with this salty snack tucked in resealable plastic bags. It makes the perfect-sized gift for little ones.

> 6 cups mini pretzels
> 6 cups fish-shaped Cheddar cheese crackers
> 3 cups cheese snack crackers
> 3 cups square rice cereal
> ½ cup butter or margarine, melted
> 2 tablespoons Worcestershire sauce
> 1½ teaspoons seasoning salt

Preheat oven to 250 degrees. In a large bowl, combine pretzels, crackers, and cereal. Combine butter, Worcestershire sauce, and seasoning salt; pour over pretzel mixture, tossing to coat. Spread mixture in a broiler pan. Bake 30 minutes, stirring twice. Cool, and store in an airtight container.
Yield: about 4½ quarts mix

People Chow

This recipe will be a big hit with the flavor combination of graham cereal, chocolate, and peanut butter.

> ½ cup butter or margarine
> 1 cup creamy peanut butter
> 1 package (11½ ounces) milk chocolate morsels
> 1 box (12 ounces) graham cereal squares
> 3 cups sifted confectioners sugar

In a large saucepan, combine butter, peanut butter, and morsels; cook over low heat, stirring constantly, until chocolate melts and mixture is smooth.

Add cereal, stirring to coat.

Place ½ of confectioners sugar in a large heavy-duty resealable plastic bag; add cereal mixture and remaining ½ of confectioners sugar. Seal bag, and gently shake to coat.

Pour mixture onto two baking sheets; let dry. Separate large pieces with a fork, if necessary. Seal in resealable plastic bags.
Yield: about 12 cups mix

Children's Party Sandwiches

Here's a great hostess favor for when children come along to an adult party. Both the hostess and the kids will love these sandwiches!

> 1 package (3 ounces) cream cheese, softened
> ¼ cup raisins
> ¼ cup unsalted dry-roasted peanuts
> 1 tablespoon milk
> Dash of ground cinnamon
> 24 slices thinly sliced wheat bread
> 1 cherry-flavored chewy fruit roll

Position knife blade in food processor bowl; add cream cheese, raisins, peanuts, milk, and cinnamon. Process until smooth.

Cut bread into 24 Christmas shapes, making a matching pair of each. Spread about 1 tablespoon filling on one side of each of 12 pieces of matching bread shapes; top with bread shape.

Unroll fruit roll; slice into 12 thin strips. Tie a bow on each sandwich.
Yield: 1 dozen sandwiches

Little Hands Can Help

Children love to help in the kitchen. Many of these recipes are easy to include the little ones in on, giving them a sense of confidence in the kitchen and creating a family team in food preparation.

Depending on the age of the children, decide what steps are best for which children to tackle. Whenever a recipe calls for combining ingredients or decorating cookies, have all the kids help out. These are safe and fun techniques for any youngster.

Colorful Christmas Balls

Colorful Christmas Balls

Let the kids get into the holiday spirit at a Christmas tree decorating party by giving them these yummy cookies to eat.

2½ cups graham cracker crumbs
1 cup sifted confectioners sugar
½ cup finely chopped pecans
½ cup candy-coated chocolate mini-morsels
1 cup flaked coconut (optional)
1 cup chocolate syrup
1½ teaspoons vanilla extract
10 squares (2 ounces each) white candy coating
Multicolored non-pareils

In a large bowl, combine crumbs, sugar, pecans, and chocolate; add coconut, if desired. Stir in syrup and vanilla.

Shape into 1-inch balls, and chill 1 hour.

Place candy coating in top of a double boiler; bring water to a boil. Reduce heat to low; cook until coating melts. Remove from heat.

Dip each ball into candy coating; place on waxed paper. Sprinkle with non-pareils.

Yield: about 4½ dozen balls

Christmas Popcorn

(pictured on page 154)

This "candied" popcorn will delight any child. Package it in an airtight plastic pail for an easy gift.

1 cup butter or margarine
¾ cup sugar
1 package (3 ounces) cherry-flavored gelatin
3 tablespoons water
1 tablespoon light corn syrup
10 cups popped popcorn

Preheat oven to 300 degrees. In a heavy 2-quart saucepan, combine butter, sugar, gelatin, water, and corn syrup; bring to a boil over medium heat, stirring constantly. Cook over medium-low heat until mixture reaches hard ball stage or candy thermometer registers 255 degrees, stirring constantly.

Place popped popcorn in a large bowl; pour hot gelatin mixture over popcorn, and stir gently until coated.

Spoon into a large baking pan. Bake 10 minutes, stirring once.

Remove to a sheet of lightly greased aluminum foil, and cool. Break into clusters. Seal in a resealable plastic bag.

Yield: about 5 cups popcorn

Chocolate Chip "Sandwich" Squares

(pictured on page 154)

Kids will gobble up their "sandwich" when you give them this chocolate chip version.

2 rolls (18 ounces each) refrigerated chocolate chip cookie dough
2 packages (8 ounces each) cream cheese, softened
1½ cups sugar
2 eggs

Freeze rolls of cookie dough for about 20 minutes; slice one roll of frozen cookie dough into 40 (⅛-inch) slices. Arrange cookie slices in a well-greased 10½ x 15½-inch jellyroll pan. Press cookie dough together to form bottom crust. Set aside.

Preheat oven to 350 degrees. Beat cream cheese at high speed of an electric mixer until fluffy; gradually add sugar, and mix well. Add eggs, 1 at a time, beating after each addition. Pour cream cheese mixture over cookie dough layer in pan.

Slice remaining frozen roll of cookie dough into 40 (⅛-inch) slices, and arrange over cream cheese mixture.

Bake 35 to 40 minutes. Cool and cut into squares.

Yield: about 3 dozen squares

Tips for Little Cooks

Read these safety tips with your child before you begin the journey into the kitchen . . . and prepare to have fun.

• Remember to wash your hands before you begin.

• Put up long hair and don't wear baggy sleeves.

• All cutting and chopping, and operation of the cooktop and oven should be done by a grown-up.

• Keep fingers away from electric mixer blades.

• Always use hot mitts when handling hot baking sheets and saucepans.

• Keep handles of pots and pans turned away from the edges of the cooktop or work area.

• If you feel uncomfortable doing something, ask a grown-up for help.

Marshmallow Cereal Pizza

Marshmallow Cereal Pizza

Take this sweet "pizza" to the neighbors' kids and watch their eyes light up. Place it in a real pizza box decorated in yuletide style.

 1 package (10½ ounces) miniature
   marshmallows
 8 ounces white candy coating, finely chopped
 ¼ cup butter or margarine
 ¼ cup light corn syrup
 6 cups crispy rice cereal
 1 cup dry-roasted peanuts
  Candy-coated chocolate pieces
  Thin red licorice

 In a heavy saucepan, combine marshmallows, candy coating, butter, and syrup; cook over low heat, stirring constantly, until smooth. Stir in cereal and peanuts. Cool to touch.

 Spoon onto an ungreased 12-inch pizza pan; shape into a circle, slightly mounding sides. Decorate with chocolate pieces and licorice, pressing into cereal mixture. Cool completely. Remove from pan.
Yield: 1 (12-inch) cereal pizza

Note: Place cellophane on the pizza pan before you put your cereal mixture on pan for easy transfer to the pizza box.

Chocolate-Peanut Butter Cups

With just two ingredients, this may be one of the easiest gifts you can make. Young and old alike relish these nuggets.

> 1 package (18 ounces) refrigerated sliceable peanut butter cookie dough
> 48 miniature peanut butter cup candies, unwrapped

Preheat oven to 350 degrees. Cut cookie dough into ¾-inch slices; cut each slice into quarters. Place quarters in greased miniature (1¾-inch) muffin pans. (Do not shape.)

Bake 9 minutes. (Dough will puff during baking.) Remove from oven, and immediately press a peanut butter cup candy gently into each cookie cup. Cool completely before removing from pans. Chill until firm.
Yield: about 4 dozen cups

Chocolate Waffle Cookies

Your waffle iron bakes these shapely little cookies that little ones will adore—no syrup needed.

> ⅓ cup vegetable shortening
> 1 square (1 ounce) unsweetened chocolate
> 1 egg, beaten
> ½ cup sugar
> 2 tablespoons milk
> ½ teaspoon vanilla extract
> ¾ cup all-purpose flour
> ½ teaspoon baking powder
> ¼ teaspoon salt
> 1 cup chopped pecans

In a saucepan, melt shortening and chocolate over low heat, stirring constantly; cool.

Combine egg, sugar, milk, and vanilla in a mixing bowl; stir well. Add chocolate mixture; stir well. Combine flour, baking powder, and salt; add to chocolate mixture, stirring well. Stir in pecans.

Preheat waffle iron at medium heat. Drop dough by level tablespoonfuls 2 inches apart onto iron. Close iron; bake 3 to 4 minutes or until done. Remove to wire racks, and cool completely.
Yield: about 2 dozen cookies

Gingerbread Animal Cookies

Half the fun of making these cookies is decorating them using tubes of frosting, so consider packaging them undecorated along with frosting tubes so the kids can get in on the action.

> ½ cup vegetable shortening
> ½ cup sugar
> ½ cup molasses
> ¼ cup water
> 2½ cups all-purpose flour
> ½ teaspoon baking soda
> ¾ teaspoon salt
> ¾ teaspoon ground ginger
> ¼ teaspoon ground nutmeg
>   Tubes of decorator frosting (optional)

Beat shortening at medium speed of an electric mixer until fluffy; gradually add sugar, beating well. Add molasses and water; beat well.

Combine flour and next 4 ingredients; add to creamed mixture, mixing well. Cover and chill dough several hours.

Preheat oven to 375 degrees. Work with ¼ of dough at a time; store remainder in refrigerator. Roll dough to ¼-inch thickness on an ungreased baking sheet. Cut with assorted 2- to 3-inch cookie cutters; remove excess dough.

Bake 6 to 8 minutes. Cool 2 minutes. Transfer to wire racks to cool. Repeat procedure with remaining dough. Decorate with colored frosting, if desired.
Yield: about 4 dozen cookies

Christmas Mice Cookies

Christmas Mice Cookies

These winsome creatures will cause a stir all through the neighborhood. They have little ears made of peanut halves, eyes of cinnamon candies, and tails of red licorice.

- ½ cup butter or margarine, softened
- 1 cup creamy peanut butter
- ½ cup firmly packed brown sugar
- ½ cup sugar
- 1 egg
- 1 teaspoon vanilla extract
- 1½ cups all-purpose flour
- ½ teaspoon baking soda
  Dry-roasted peanuts
- 1 jar (2.25 ounces) small red cinnamon candies
- 4 yards thin red licorice, cut into 3-inch pieces

In a large mixing bowl, beat butter and peanut butter at medium speed of an electric mixer until creamy; gradually add sugars, beating well. Add egg and vanilla, beating well.

Combine flour and baking soda; gradually add to butter mixture, beating until blended. Cover and chill at least 2 hours.

Preheat oven to 350 degrees. Shape dough into 1-inch balls; taper one end of each ball to form a teardrop shape. Press one side flat; place cookies, flat sides down, 2 inches apart on ungreased baking sheets. Gently press in sides of dough to raise backs of mice. Gently place 2 peanut halves in dough for ears. With a wooden pick, make a ½-inch-deep hole at tail end.

Bake 9 minutes. Remove from oven, and carefully place red cinnamon candies in cookies for eyes. Return to oven, and bake 1 to 2 more minutes or until browned. Remove from oven; insert licorice tails. Cool on baking sheets on wire racks.
Yield: about 4 dozen cookies

Santa's Boot Cookies

(pictured on page 154)

Writing names on Santa's Boot Cookies is a great way to personalize a gift for children and make them feel extra special.

- 1 package (18 ounces) refrigerated sliceable sugar cookie dough
- 2 cups confectioners sugar
- 2 tablespoons lemon juice
- 2 tablespoons water
  Red paste food coloring
  Decorator Frosting

Divide dough in half; store one portion in refrigerator. Roll dough to ¼-inch thickness on floured waxed paper on a baking sheet. Cut with a 2½- to 3-inch boot-shaped cookie cutter, and freeze 10 minutes.

Remove dough from freezer, and transfer to ungreased baking sheets. Bake according to package directions. Transfer to wire racks to cool. Repeat procedure with remaining dough.

Combine confectioners sugar, lemon juice, and water, stirring until smooth. Tint about ⅔ of glaze with red food coloring.

Use a small brush to paint top of boot with white glaze and bottom of boot with red glaze.

Spoon Decorator Frosting into a decorating bag fitted with metal tip No. 2; pipe an outline and names on cookies.
Yield: about 2½ dozen cookies

Decorator Frosting

- 1½ tablespoons butter or margarine, softened
- 1 cup confectioners sugar
- 1 tablespoon milk
- ¼ teaspoon vanilla extract

In a small mixing bowl, beat butter at medium speed of an electric mixer until creamy; add sugar and milk, beating until spreading consistency. Stir in vanilla.
Yield: about ½ cup frosting

Jam-Filled Snowmen

What a whimsical treat for kids! Give these cookies in a fun cookie jar that can be used year-round. Attach a copy of the recipe to the jar.

- ½ cup butter or margarine, softened
- 1 cup sugar
- 1 egg
- 2 cups all-purpose flour
- ¾ teaspoon baking powder
- ¼ teaspoon salt
- 1 teaspoon ground cinnamon
- ¼ cup milk
  Confectioners sugar
- ⅔ cup seedless raspberry jam

In a large mixing bowl, beat butter at medium speed of an electric mixer until creamy; gradually add 1 cup sugar, beating mixture well. Add egg, beating well.

Combine flour and next 3 ingredients in a bowl; add to butter mixture alternately with milk, beginning and ending with flour mixture. Cover and chill 1 hour.

Preheat oven to 375 degrees. Roll dough to ⅛-inch thickness on a well floured surface. Cut with a 4-inch snowman-shaped cookie cutter, and place 2 inches apart on greased baking sheets.

Use a 1-inch heart-shaped cutter to cut out a heart in ½ of cookies; place heart in hand of snowman.

Bake 5 to 8 minutes or until lightly browned around edges. Transfer to wire racks to cool.

Sprinkle cutout cookies with confectioners sugar. Spread solid cookies with raspberry jam; top with cutout cookies.

Yield: about 3 dozen cookies

Chewy Chocolate Cereal Bars

Delight your young neighbors with this easy-to-make chocolaty twist on a favorite sweet snack.

- 1 can (14 ounces) chocolate sweetened condensed milk
- 1 package (10 ounces) peanut butter morsels
- 1 package (10½ ounces) miniature marshmallows
- 1 package (15 ounces) toasted oat cereal (13 cups)
- 1 cup chopped roasted peanuts

In a Dutch oven, cook milk, morsels, and marshmallows over medium heat, stirring constantly, 7 minutes or until melted and smooth.

Stir in cereal and peanuts. Press into a lightly greased 10½ x 15½-inch jellyroll pan or 2 (9-inch) square pans. Cool 3 hours or until firm. Cut into bars.
Yield: about 2 dozen bars

Cracker Candy

The adults will want this treat for themselves, so you may want to make two batches! Package this candy in paper cones tied with ribbon for a colorful surprise.

- 2½ cups miniature round butter-flavored crackers
- ¾ cup butter
- ¾ cup firmly packed brown sugar
- 1 package (12 ounces) milk chocolate morsels
  Chopped pecans (optional)
  Multicolored candy sprinkles (optional)

Preheat oven to 350 degrees. Place crackers in a lightly greased aluminum foil-lined 9 x 13-inch pan.

Bring butter and brown sugar to a boil in a medium saucepan, stirring constantly; cook, stirring often, 3 minutes. Pour mixture over crackers.

Bake 5 minutes. Turn oven off. Sprinkle crackers with chocolate morsels, and let stand in oven 3 minutes or until chocolate melts. Spread melted chocolate evenly over crackers. Top with pecans or candy sprinkles, if desired. Cool and break into pieces. Store in refrigerator.
Yield: about 10 servings

Note: You can freeze cookies up to 6 months before decorating.

Cracker Candy

Ultimate Chocolate Gifts

Here you'll find our most decadent chocolate recipes. From cookies to cheesecake, find a present suited for the person with a passion for chocolate.

Black and White Torta, page 176; Chocolate Mocha Crunch Pie, page 175

Chocolate Cheese Ball

Chocolate Cheese Ball

This cheese ball is a twist on the traditional party starter—chock full of chocolate.

> 1 package (8 ounces) cream cheese, softened
> ¼ cup butter or margarine, softened
> ¾ cup confectioners sugar
> 2 tablespoons light brown sugar
> 3 tablespoons cocoa
> 1 tablespoon Kahlúa or amaretto
> ½ cup semisweet chocolate morsels
> ½ cup finely chopped pecans

In a medium bowl, combine cream cheese and butter; beating until well blended. Stir in sugars, cocoa, and liqueur. Stir in morsels. Cover and refrigerate overnight or up to 3 days.

Shape mixture into a ball and roll in pecans.

Yield: 1 cheese ball

Directions for gift card: Store in refrigerator up to 3 days. Serve with graham crackers, cookies, or sliced fruit.

White Chocolate-Macadamia Nut Cookies

Macadamia nuts seem like they were made to be combined with white chocolate—making a perfectly rich cookie.

> ½ cup butter or margarine, softened
> ½ cup vegetable shortening
> ¾ cup firmly packed brown sugar
> ½ cup sugar
> 1 egg
> 1½ teaspoons vanilla extract
> 2 cups all-purpose flour
> 1 teaspoon baking soda
> ½ teaspoon salt
> 1 package (6 ounces) white chocolate-flavored baking bars, cut into chunks
> 1 jar (7 ounces) macadamia nuts, chopped

Preheat oven to 350 degrees. Beat butter and shortening at medium speed of an electric mixer until creamy; gradually add sugars, beating well. Add egg and vanilla; beat well. Combine flour, baking soda, and salt; gradually add to butter mixture, beating well. Stir in white chocolate and nuts.

Drop dough by rounded teaspoonfuls 2 inches apart onto lightly greased baking sheets. Bake 8 to 10 minutes or until lightly browned. Cool slightly on baking sheets; remove to wire racks to cool completely.

Yield: about 5 dozen cookies

Tiger Cookies

Corn flake cereal yields a mighty crunch in these crispy cookies.

> ¾ cup butter-flavored vegetable shortening
> 1 cup firmly packed brown sugar
> 2 eggs
> 1 teaspoon vanilla extract
> 2 cups all-purpose flour
> 1 teaspoon baking powder
> ½ teaspoon salt
> ½ teaspoon ground cinnamon
> 3 cups sugar-coated corn flake cereal, slightly crushed
> 1 cup (6 ounces) milk chocolate morsels, melted and cooled to room temperature

Preheat oven to 350 degrees. In a large mixing bowl, beat shortening at medium speed of an electric mixer until creamy. Gradually add sugar, beating until blended. Add eggs, 1 at a time, beating well after each addition. Stir in vanilla.

Combine flour and next 3 ingredients; stir well. Add to sugar mixture, blending well. Stir in cereal.

Drizzle ½ of chocolate over dough; stir lightly. Drizzle remaining chocolate over dough; stir lightly, leaving streaks of chocolate. Drop dough by heaping teaspoonfuls 2 inches apart onto ungreased baking sheets. Bake 8 to 10 minutes or until golden. Remove to wire racks to cool.

Yield: about 5 dozen cookies

Caramel-Filled Chocolate Cookies

These delicious caramel-surprise cookies are great warm or cool—so you can eat a couple when you bake them and package the rest for a gift.

- 1 cup butter or margarine
- 1 cup granulated sugar
- 1 cup firmly packed brown sugar
- 2 eggs
- 2 teaspoons vanilla extract
- 2¼ cups all-purpose flour
- 1 teaspoon baking soda
- ¾ cup cocoa
- 1 cup finely chopped walnuts, divided
- 1 tablespoon granulated sugar
- 1 package (9 ounces) chocolate-covered caramels

Beat butter at medium speed of an electric mixer until creamy; gradually add sugars, beating well. Add eggs and vanilla; beat well.

Combine flour, baking soda, and cocoa; gradually add to butter mixture, beating well. Stir in ½ cup walnuts. Cover and chill dough at least 2 hours. Combine remaining ½ cup walnuts and 1 tablespoon sugar.

Divide dough into 4 equal portions. Work with one portion at a time, storing remainder in refrigerator.

Preheat oven to 375 degrees. Divide each portion into 12 pieces. Quickly press each piece of dough around a caramel; roll into a ball. Dip one side of ball in walnut mixture. Place balls, walnut side up, 2 inches apart on ungreased baking sheets.

Bake 8 minutes. (Cookies will look soft.) Cool 1 minute on baking sheets; remove to wire racks to cool.

Yield: about 4 dozen cookies

Spicy Cocoa Snaps

Dark rum and coriander add a surprising Caribbean flair to these slice-and-bake cookies.

- 1½ cups all-purpose flour
- ¾ cup cocoa
- 1 teaspoon ground cinnamon
- ¼ teaspoon salt
- ¼ teaspoon ground coriander
- ¼ teaspoon ground nutmeg
- ¼ teaspoon ground cloves
- ⅛ teaspoon pepper
- ¾ cup butter, softened
- 1 cup sugar
- 1 egg
- 2 tablespoons dark rum

In a medium bowl, combine first 8 ingredients; stir well. Beat butter in a large bowl at medium speed of an electric mixer until creamy; gradually add sugar, beating well. Add egg, beating until blended. Stir in rum. Gradually add flour mixture, beating just until blended after each addition. Cover and chill dough 45 minutes.

Shape dough into a 13-inch log on waxed paper; wrap and freeze log 1 hour or until firm, or up to 1 month.

Preheat oven to 350 degrees. Cut frozen log into ¼-inch slices, and place on lightly greased baking sheets. Bake 12 minutes. Remove to wire racks to cool completely.

Yield: about 4 dozen cookies

Spicy Cocoa Snaps

Chocolate-Caramel Brownies

These brownies will not look done because of gooey caramel in the middle. Refrigerate them before cutting.

- 1 box (18.25 ounces) German or other chocolate cake mix
- ¾ cup butter or margarine, melted
- ⅔ cup evaporated milk, divided
- 1 cup pecans, chopped
- 1 package (14 ounces) chocolate-covered caramels or plain caramels
- 1 cup (6 ounces) semisweet chocolate morsels

Preheat oven to 350 degrees. In a large bowl, combine cake mix, butter, ⅓ cup evaporated milk, and pecans, stirring with a spoon until dough forms. Press ½ of dough into a well-greased 9 x 13-inch pan and bake 6 minutes, reserving remaining dough.

In a medium saucepan, melt caramels with remaining milk over medium heat, stirring frequently. Remove pan from oven and sprinkle chocolate morsels over hot dough; spread melted caramel mixture over chocolate, then crumble remaining dough over top. Bake 20 more minutes. Cool; chill at least 1 hour before cutting.

Yield: about 1 dozen brownies

Chewy Brownie Grahams

You won't believe these fudgy-chewy brownies have only five ingredients. The thick batter is loaded with chocolate cookie crumbs.

- 1 cup (6 ounces) semisweet chocolate morsels
- ½ cup creamy or chunky peanut butter
- 1 can (14 ounces) sweetened condensed milk
- ½ cup coarsely chopped pecans, toasted
- 2 cups chocolate graham cracker crumbs or chocolate wafer cookie crumbs

Preheat oven to 350 degrees. In a large heavy saucepan, combine morsels, peanut butter, and milk; cook over medium heat, stirring constantly, until morsels and peanut butter melt. Remove from heat.

Stir in pecans and chocolate crumbs. (Batter will be very thick.) Press batter into a well-greased 8-inch square pan. Bake 24 minutes. Cool in pan on a wire rack. Cut into 2-inch squares.

Yield: about 16 brownies

Chocolate-Caramel Brownies

Double Chocolate Espresso Brownies

Anyone who craves the rich combination of coffee and chocolate will find these brownies irresistible!

 Butter-flavored cooking spray
1¼ cups all-purpose flour
 ¼ teaspoon baking soda
 ⅛ teaspoon baking powder
 ⅛ teaspoon salt
14 squares (1 ounce each) semisweet chocolate, finely chopped
 1 cup sugar
 ½ cup butter or margarine
 ¼ cup light corn syrup
 ¼ cup espresso or strongly brewed French roast coffee, cooled
 3 eggs
 1 tablespoon vanilla extract
 1 cup chopped walnuts
 6 ounces premium Swiss dark or milk chocolate, coarsely chopped

Preheat oven to 325 degrees. Coat a 9 x 13-inch pan with cooking spray. Line pan with aluminum foil, allowing ends to hang over short sides of pan. Tuck overlapping ends under rim on short sides. Coat foil with cooking spray; set pan aside.

In a small bowl, combine flour and next 3 ingredients. Place chopped semisweet chocolate in a large bowl; set aside.

Combine sugar and next 3 ingredients in a saucepan; cook over medium heat, stirring constantly, until sugar and butter melt and mixture comes to a rolling boil. Remove from heat, and pour over chopped chocolate in bowl; let stand 2 minutes. (Do not stir.)

Beat mixture at low speed of an electric mixer until chocolate melts and mixture is smooth. Add eggs, 1 at a time, beating well after each addition. Add flour mixture; beat at medium speed until well blended. Stir in vanilla, walnuts, and dark chocolate.

Spoon batter into prepared pan, spreading evenly. Bake 45 to 48 minutes. Cool completely in pan on a wire rack. Cover brownies with overlapping foil; chill at least 2 hours.

Carefully invert brownies from pan, using overlapping foil as handles; remove foil. Invert brownies again onto a cutting board; cut into squares or diamonds.
Yield: about 4 dozen brownies

Fudge Puddles

These candies with a rich fudge filling give new meaning to gooey.

 ½ cup butter or margarine, softened
 ½ cup creamy peanut butter
 ½ cup sugar
 ½ cup firmly packed light brown sugar
 1 egg
 ½ teaspoon vanilla extract
1¼ cups all-purpose flour
 ¾ teaspoon baking soda
 ½ teaspoon salt
 Fudge Filling
 Chopped peanuts

Beat butter and peanut butter at medium speed of an electric mixer until creamy; gradually add sugars, beating well. Add egg and vanilla, beat well.

Combine flour, baking soda, and salt; gradually add to butter mixture. Cover and chill dough.

Preheat oven to 325 degrees. Shape dough into 1-inch balls. Press into lightly greased miniature (1¾-inch) muffin pans.

Bake 16 minutes. Immediately make indentations in center of each ball by lightly pressing with the back of a melon ball cutter or other round tool.

Cool in pan 5 minutes; remove to wire racks to cool completely. Spoon Fudge Filling into centers. Sprinkle with chopped peanuts.
Yield: about 3 dozen cookies

Fudge Filling

 1 cup milk chocolate morsels
 1 cup semisweet chocolate morsels
 1 can (14 ounces) sweetened condensed milk
 1 teaspoon vanilla extract

Melt chocolate morsels in a heavy saucepan over low heat, stirring until smooth. Remove from heat; stir in milk and vanilla.
Yield: about 2 cups filling

Caramel Fudge Cutouts

Nothing says Christmas like a gift of fudge—caramel makes these cutouts simply irresistible!

- 2 cups sugar
- ¼ cup cocoa
- ¾ cup milk
- 2 tablespoons light corn syrup
- ¼ cup plus 2 tablespoons butter, divided
- 8 caramels, chopped
- ¾ cup chopped skinned hazelnuts or pecans
- 2 teaspoons vanilla extract

Line a 9-inch square pan with aluminum foil, allowing foil to extend over edges of pan. Butter foil; set aside.

Butter insides of a heavy 3-quart saucepan. Combine sugar and cocoa in saucepan, stirring well.

Stir in milk and corn syrup. Bring to a boil over medium-low heat, stirring gently and constantly with a wooden spoon, until sugar dissolves (6 to 8 minutes). Add ¼ cup butter, stirring until butter melts. Cover and boil 3 minutes over medium heat.

Uncover and cook, without stirring, until candy thermometer registers 238 degrees (about 14 minutes). Remove from heat. Add remaining 2 tablespoons butter, chopped caramels, nuts, and vanilla. Do not stir. Cool mixture to 130 degrees (about 25 minutes).

Beat fudge by hand with a wooden spoon until it thickens and begins to lose its gloss (10 minutes). Quickly spread fudge into prepared pan; cool (about 3 hours). Lift uncut fudge out of pan with foil; discard foil, and place fudge on a cutting board. Cut desired shapes, using 2-inch cookie cutters, or cut fudge into 1½-inch squares.

Yield: about 16 cutouts or about 3 dozen squares

Caramel Fudge Cutouts

Chocolate Truffles

Truffles make wonderful gifts given in small paper baking cups layered in a tin.

- ⅔ cup heavy whipping cream
- 3 tablespoons unsalted butter, cut into chunks
- 2 tablespoons sugar
- 1 tablespoon flavored liqueur
- 8 ounces Baker's German baking chocolate, cut into chunks
  Coatings: Unsweetened cocoa, shredded coconut, and ground assorted nuts

In a medium saucepan, bring cream, butter, and sugar to a full boil over medium heat, stirring constantly. Remove from heat. Add liqueur and chocolate. Stir until chocolate melts and mixture is smooth; chill until firm enough to handle (about 3 hours). Shape into 1-inch balls and roll in your favorite coating. Store in refrigerator.
Yield: about 2 dozen truffles

Directions for gift card: Store in refrigerator up to 5 days.

Hot Chocolate Muffins

A basket of these muffins will be welcomed with open arms.

- 2¼ cups biscuit and baking mix
- ½ cup sugar
- 2 tablespoons cocoa
- ½ cup half and half
- ¼ cup chocolate syrup
- 3 tablespoons vegetable oil
- 2 teaspoons vanilla extract
- 1 egg, lightly beaten
- ¾ cup semisweet chocolate mini-morsels
- ¼ cup sliced almonds

Preheat oven to 400 degrees. In a large bowl, combine baking mix, sugar, and cocoa. Make a well in center of mixture. Combine half and half and next 4 ingredients; add to dry ingredients, stirring just until dry ingredients are moistened. Stir in chocolate morsels and almonds. Spoon into greased muffin pans, filling two-thirds full. Bake 11 to 12 minutes or until a wooden pick inserted in center of muffin comes out clean. Remove from pans immediately.
Yield: about 1 dozen muffins

German Chocolate Sauce

Searching for the perfect chocolate sauce? Look no further than this silky concoction.

- ½ cup butter
- 1 package (4 ounces) sweet baking chocolate
- 1½ cups sugar
- 1 teaspoon vanilla extract
- ⅛ teaspoon salt
- 1 can (5 ounces) evaporated milk

Melt butter and chocolate in a small saucepan over low heat, stirring until melted.
Stir in sugar, vanilla, salt, and milk; bring to a boil over medium heat. Cook 7 minutes, stirring constantly.
Yield: about 2 cups sauce

Directions for gift card: Store sauce in refrigerator. Reheat sauce in a microwave oven at medium power (50%). (Time will vary with amount of sauce.) Serve warm over ice cream or pound cake.

Chocolate Decorations

From simple grated chocolate to elaborate chocolate curls, you can depend on this indulgent confection for pretty garnishes. Here's how:

Grated Chocolate: Grate unsweetened, semisweet, or milk chocolate to sprinkle on top of pies, cakes, or other desserts. Use a food processor for quick grating or create the garnish by hand. When grating by hand, be sure to hold the chocolate with a paper towel or waxed paper so the heat of your hand won't melt the chocolate.

Chocolate Curls: Melt 4 (1-ounce) squares semisweet chocolate over hot water in a double boiler. Pour chocolate onto a waxed paper-lined baking sheet. Spread chocolate with a spatula into a 3-inch-wide strip. Smooth top with a spatula. Chill chocolate until it feels slightly tacky but not firm. (If too hard, curls will break; if too soft, chocolate will not curl.)

Gently pull a vegetable peeler across chocolate until curls form. Transfer curls to a tray by inserting a wooden pick in end of curl. Chill curls until ready to use.

Chocolate Mocha Trifle

Chocolate Mocha Trifle

This trifle makes an elegant gift for a holiday gathering. Make the trifle dish, tied with a big red bow, a part of the gift.

 1 package (19.8 ounces) brownie mix
 4 teaspoons instant coffee granules
1¾ cup cold milk
 2 packages (3.3 ounces each) white chocolate instant pudding mix
 1 container (12 ounces) frozen non-dairy whipped topping, thawed
 Crushed chocolate-covered toffee bars or fresh sliced strawberries (optional)

Bake brownies according to package directions; cool. Cut into bite-sized squares. Combine coffee granules and milk; stir well until coffee is dissolved. Stir pudding mix and milk mixture 4 minutes or until thickened. Fold in whipped topping; chill. Layer in a glass bowl in following order: brownies, pudding mix, and toffee or strawberries, if desired; repeat layers.
Yield: about 16 servings

Directions for gift card: Store in refrigerator until ready to serve.

Chocolate Mocha Crunch Pie

(pictured on page 166)

The crunch in this pie comes from a wonderful crust made with pie crust mix, grated chocolate, and walnuts.

 Mocha Pastry Shell
 1 square (1 ounce) unsweetened chocolate, chopped
⅓ cup butter or margarine
¾ cup firmly packed brown sugar
¼ cup all-purpose flour
 2 teaspoons instant coffee granules
1½ cups milk
 2 egg yolks, lightly beaten
 2 cups whipping cream
½ cup sifted confectioners sugar
1½ tablespoons instant coffee granules
 Chocolate-covered coffee beans, chopped (optional)

Prepare Mocha Pastry Shell; set aside.
Place 1 square chopped chocolate and butter in top of a double boiler; bring water to a boil. Reduce heat to low; stir in brown sugar, flour, and 2 teaspoons coffee granules. Gradually stir in milk, and cook 10 minutes or until mixture thickens.

Gradually add ¼ of hot mixture to egg yolks. Add to remaining hot mixture, stirring constantly. Cook, stirring constantly, 20 to 25 minutes or until mixture is very thick. Remove from heat. Pour filling into cooled pastry shell. Cover; chill at least 6 hours.
About 1 or 2 hours before serving, beat whipping cream, confectioners sugar, and 1½ tablespoons coffee granules in a large chilled mixing bowl at medium speed of an electric mixer until soft peaks form. (Do not overbeat.) Spoon over chilled filling. Sprinkle with chopped coffee beans, if desired. Chill.
Yield: about 8 servings

Mocha Pastry Shell

 1 pie crust stick, crumbled or ½ (11-ounce) package pie crust mix
 1 square (1 ounce) unsweetened chocolate, grated
¾ cup finely chopped walnuts
¼ cup firmly packed brown sugar
 2 tablespoons water
 1 teaspoon vanilla extract

Preheat oven to 375 degrees. In a medium bowl, use a fork to combine crumbled pie crust stick and chocolate. Stir in walnuts and brown sugar. Combine water and vanilla; sprinkle over pastry mixture. Mix with fork until mixture forms a ball.
Line a 9-inch pie plate with aluminum foil. Line bottom with waxed paper. Spray waxed paper and foil with cooking spray. Press pastry mixture evenly into pie plate.
Bake 15 minutes; cool completely. Invert crust onto another pie plate; remove foil. Return to 9-inch pie plate.
Yield: 1 (9-inch) pastry shell

Directions for gift card: Store in refrigerator until ready to serve.

Mint Chocolate Mousse Pie

Mint Chocolate Mousse Pie

This pie looks like a fancy chocolate creation—but it's quick and convenient because it's made with a cheese-cake mix.

> 1 package (11.1 ounces) no-bake cheesecake mix
> ⅓ cup butter or margarine, melted
> 2 tablespoons sugar
> 1 cup milk
> ½ cup chocolate mint-flavored syrup
> 2 minty milk chocolate bars with crunchy cookie bits (1.55 ounces each), finely chopped
> Sweetened whipped cream and additional chopped chocolate bars to garnish

Combine graham cracker crumbs from cheesecake mix, butter, and sugar. Firmly press mixture in bottom and up sides of a 9-inch pie plate.

Combine milk and chocolate syrup in a medium bowl, stirring well. Add cheesecake filling mix; beat at low speed of an electric mixer until blended. Beat at medium speed 3 minutes. Fold in finely chopped chocolate. Spoon into prepared crust. Cover and chill at least 1 hour. Garnish, if desired.
Yield: 1 (9-inch) pie

Directions for gift card: Chill pie at least 4 hours before serving. When ready to serve, dip bottom of pie plate in hot water for 30 seconds.

Black and White Torta
(pictured on page 166)

This silky, creamy dessert, with its elegant chocolate shavings, is sure to please any recipient.

> 2 cups graham cracker crumbs
> ½ cup cocoa
> 1 cup sugar
> ½ cup unsalted butter or margarine, melted
> Dark Chocolate Filling
> White Chocolate Filling
> Chocolate shavings or curls to garnish

Preheat oven to 350 degrees. Combine first 4 ingredients. Press over bottom and 1 inch up sides of a 10-inch springform pan. Bake 5 minutes on center rack of oven. Cool on a wire rack.

Prepare Dark Chocolate Filling; pour into prepared pan; cover and chill 30 minutes. Meanwhile, prepare White Chocolate Filling; pour over chilled dark chocolate layer. Cover and chill at least 8 hours.

Run a knife around sides of pan to loosen torta. Place on a gift platter, and remove sides of pan. Garnish, if desired.
Yield: 16 to 18 servings

Dark Chocolate Filling

16 squares (1 ounce each) bittersweet chocolate, coarsely chopped
1½ cups whipping cream

Place chocolate and cream in top of a double boiler. Place over warm, but not simmering, water, and cook, stirring occasionally, until chocolate melts.
Yield: about 2¾ cups filling

White Chocolate Filling

4 packages (4 ounces each) white chocolate, coarsely chopped
3 cups whipping cream, divided
2 teaspoons unflavored gelatin
2 tablespoons cold water
1½ teaspoons vanilla extract

Combine white chocolate and 1 cup cream in top of a double boiler. Place over warm, but not simmering, water; cook, stirring occasionally, until chocolate melts. Remove from heat and cool 5 minutes. Set aside.

Sprinkle gelatin over cold water in a small saucepan; let stand 1 minute. Cook over low heat, stirring until gelatin dissolves. Remove from heat and cool 2 minutes.

Beat remaining 2 cups whipping cream and vanilla at medium speed of an electric mixer until soft peaks form, gradually adding cooled white chocolate mixture and dissolved gelatin. Increase to high speed, and beat until mixture begins to thicken and soft peaks form (about 5 minutes).
Yield: about 6 cups filling

Directions for gift card: Store in refrigerator until ready to serve.

Chocolate Linzertorte

This elegant torte, which originated in Linz, Austria, boasts a raspberry jam filling encased in a buttery chocolate-almond lattice crust.

¾ cup butter, softened
½ cup sugar
3 egg yolks
2 cups all-purpose flour
¼ teaspoon salt
1 teaspoon ground allspice
3 squares (1 ounce each) semisweet chocolate, melted and cooled
1½ cups whole natural almonds, toasted and ground
1 cup seedless raspberry jam
1 package (6 ounces) semisweet chocolate morsels

Beat butter at medium speed of an electric mixer until soft and creamy; gradually add sugar, beating well. Add egg yolks, beating well.

Combine flour, salt, and allspice; add to butter mixture alternately with melted chocolate, beginning and ending with flour mixture. Stir in almonds. Divide dough in half.

Preheat oven to 375 degrees. Roll ½ of dough between 2 sheets of waxed paper to an 11-inch circle. Freeze 15 minutes. Press remaining ½ of dough into a greased 11-inch tart pan.

Bake 5 minutes. Stir jam well and spread over crust. Sprinkle with chocolate morsels.

Remove top sheet of waxed paper from frozen circle of dough; cut into ½-inch-wide strips, using a fluted pastry wheel. Arrange strips in lattice design over torte, sealing ends of strips to prebaked crust.

Bake at 375 degrees for 20 to 25 minutes. Cool completely in pan on a wire rack.
Yield: 1 (11-inch) torte

Directions for gift card: Serve torte at room temperature with whipped cream.

Almond Macaroon Tart

You'll think you're eating a candy bar when you take a bite of this dessert laden with coconut, almonds, and chocolate.

- 1¼ cups chocolate wafer crumbs
- 1 cup sliced almonds, ground
- ¼ cup butter or margarine, melted
- 2 egg whites
- ⅓ cup sugar
- 1 package (7 ounces) flaked coconut
- ⅓ cup sweetened condensed milk
- 1 teaspoon vanilla extract
- ¼ cup butter or margarine
- 3 squares (1 ounce each) unsweetened chocolate, chopped
- 3 eggs
- ½ cup sugar
- ⅛ teaspoon salt
- 1 teaspoon vanilla extract
- 1 cup whole natural almonds
- 10 squares (1 ounce each) semisweet chocolate, divided
- ½ cup whipping cream
- 1 tablespoon light corn syrup
- 1 square (1 ounce) white chocolate, chopped
- 1½ teaspoons vegetable shortening

Preheat oven to 350 degrees. Combine first 3 ingredients in a bowl, stirring well. Pat mixture onto bottom and sides of a lightly greased 11-inch tart pan. Bake 10 minutes.

Beat egg whites at high speed of an electric mixer until soft peaks form. Gradually add ⅓ cup sugar, beating 4 minutes or until thickened. Stir in coconut, sweetened condensed milk, and 1 teaspoon vanilla. Spread coconut mixture over crust in pan.

Melt ¼ cup butter and unsweetened chocolate in a heavy saucepan over medium-low heat. Remove from heat.

Beat 3 eggs at medium speed until thick and frothy. Gradually add ½ cup sugar, salt, and 1 teaspoon vanilla, beating until blended. Stir in melted chocolate mixture. Spoon over coconut mixture in tart pan.

Bake 40 minutes. Cool completely; carefully remove sides of tart pan.

Roast whole almonds on a baking sheet at 350 degrees for 8 to 12 minutes. Cool. Melt 4 ounces semisweet chocolate in top of a double boiler over hot, but not simmering, water. Remove from heat and cool until chocolate registers 90 degrees on an instant-read thermometer. Add roasted almonds, stirring constantly for 2 to 3 minutes until chocolate begins to set. Remove chocolate-coated almonds and let dry on waxed paper.

Bring whipping cream and corn syrup to a boil in a small saucepan. Remove from heat and pour over remaining 6 ounces semisweet chocolate. Let stand 1 minute. Whisk until smooth. Pour chocolate mixture over baked tart. Place chocolate-coated almonds around edge of tart.

Melt white chocolate and shortening in top of double boiler over hot, but not simmering, water. Remove from heat and drizzle over tart. Let stand until topping is set.

Yield: 1 (11-inch) tart

Satiny Mocha Torte

Convenience products do most of the work in this stunning four-layer cake with a shiny chocolate top. Remind the recipient to store this luscious mousse-filled cake in the refrigerator.

- ¾ cup whole hazelnuts in the skins
- 1 package (18.25 ounces) devil's food cake mix without pudding
- 2 packages (2.8 ounces each) mocha mousse mix
- 1⅓ cups milk
- ¾ cup whipping cream
- 1½ tablespoons Swiss-style flavored instant coffee powder
- 6 squares (1 ounce each) semisweet chocolate, chopped

Preheat oven to 350 degrees. Place hazelnuts in an ungreased 10½ x 15½-inch jellyroll pan. Toast 12 minutes or until skins begin to split. Transfer hot nuts to a colander; cover with a kitchen towel. Rub nuts briskly with towel to remove skins. Cool nuts, and chop.

Grease and flour 2 (9-inch) cake pans. Prepare cake mix according to package directions; pour into prepared pans. Bake 30 minutes or until a wooden pick inserted in center of cake comes out clean. Cool in pans on wire racks 15 minutes; remove from pans, and cool completely on wire racks.

Prepare mousse mix according to package directions, using 1⅓ cups milk; cover and chill.

Split cake layers in half horizontally to make 4 layers. Place one layer on a serving plate lined with waxed paper. Spread ⅓ of mousse over layer. Repeat procedure with second and third layers and remaining mousse. Top stack with fourth layer. Chill 30 minutes.

Combine whipping cream and coffee powder in a saucepan; bring to a simmer over medium heat. Remove from heat; add chocolate. Let stand 1 minute. Stir until chocolate melts. Cool 30 minutes.

Pour chocolate glaze over torte, letting excess drip down sides onto waxed paper. Using a small spatula, smooth excess glaze onto sides of torte. Gently press hazelnuts onto sides of glazed torte. Carefully pull waxed paper from beneath torte. Store in refrigerator.

Yield: 1 (9-inch) torte

Satiny Mocha Torte

Chocolate White Chocolate Cheesecake

Cheesecake this chocolaty could be dangerous—unless you're a true chocoholic.

28 cream-filled chocolate sandwich cookies
1½ cups sugar, divided
6 tablespoons unsalted butter or margarine, melted
5 packages (8 ounces each) cream cheese, softened
¼ cup all-purpose flour
5 eggs
2 egg yolks
1 teaspoon vanilla extract
8 squares (1 ounce each) white baking chocolate, chopped (we tested with Ghirardelli)
¼ cup half and half
    Chocolate curls to garnish

Position knife blade in food processor bowl; add cookies and ¼ cup sugar. Process until finely ground. Add butter; process until well blended, stopping once to scrape down sides. Firmly press crumb mixture on bottom and 1 inch up sides of a greased 10-inch springform pan. Chill 1 hour.

Preheat oven to 325 degrees. Beat cream cheese at medium speed of an electric mixer until creamy. Combine remaining 1¼ cups sugar and flour. Gradually add sugar mixture to cream cheese, beating well. Add eggs and yolks, 1 at a time, beating after each addition. Stir in vanilla, white chocolate, and half and half. Pour mixture into prepared crust.

Bake 1 hour and 15 minutes or until cheesecake is almost set. Turn oven off, and partially open oven door; leave cheesecake in oven 30 minutes. Cool to room temperature in pan on a wire rack. Cover and chill at least 8 hours. Remove sides of pan. Garnish, if desired.
Yield: about 12 servings

Directions for gift card: Store in refrigerator until ready to serve.

Mini-Mexican Chocolate Soufflé Cakes

What a party pleaser! A tray full of cakes ready to be enjoyed.

1 bar (8 ounces) semisweet chocolate, chopped
½ cup unsalted butter, cut into 1-inch pieces
1½ teaspoons instant espresso powder
⅛ teaspoon salt
6 egg yolks
⅓ cup sugar
1 teaspoon vanilla extract
1 teaspoon ground cinnamon
2 egg whites
    Confectioners sugar
    Fresh strawberries and mint sprigs to garnish

Grease 6 (4½-inch-diameter) tartlet pans with ¾-inch-high sides and removable bottoms. Place tartlet pans on a baking sheet.

In a heavy medium saucepan, stir chocolate and butter over low heat until melted and smooth. Remove from heat. Add espresso powder and salt; stir to blend well. Cool to lukewarm, stirring occasionally.

Using electric mixer, beat egg yolks, all but 1 tablespoon sugar, vanilla, and cinnamon in a large bowl until mixture is thick, about 5 minutes. Stir ¼ of egg mixture into chocolate mixture. Fold chocolate mixture into remaining egg mixture. Beat egg whites in another large bowl until soft peaks form. Add 1 tablespoon sugar; beat just until stiff peaks form. Fold into chocolate mixture. Divide batter among prepared pans. Place pans on a foil-lined baking sheet. Cover; chill at least 1 hour and up to 4 hours.

Position rack in center of oven and preheat oven to 400 degrees. Bake cakes until edges are set and centers are still soft, about 13 minutes. Cool on racks 2 minutes.

Run knife around pan sides to loosen cakes. Remove pan sides and bottoms, and cool cakes completely on wire racks. Transfer cooled cakes to a tray or gift plate. Dust cakes lightly with confectioners sugar. Top each cake with a fanned, sliced strawberry and a sprig of mint, if desired.
Yield: 6 cakes

Chocolate Storage Suggestions

Store chocolate tightly wrapped in a cool, dry place. In hot weather, you can refrigerate it, but wrap it in foil and seal in a plastic bag so it doesn't absorb other food flavors. Let it return to room temperature still wrapped so moisture doesn't condense on it. Moisture can cause chocolate to lump when melted.

Occasionally, there may be a slight graying or "bloom" on chocolate. This does not alter the quality or flavor and when used in a recipe, the chocolate will regain its color.

Mini-Mexican
Chocolate Soufflé Cakes

Mini-Mexican Chocolate Soufflé Cakes

Favorite Gifts and a Make-Ahead Plan

Keep track of gift giving with this handy list. And use the monthly planning space on the opposite page to help plan gifts you want to make ahead.

Gift List

Name	Gift	Sent/Delivered

July

Examples: Herbed Steak Rub, page 91 ....

Chowchow, page 85 ....

....

....

....

....

....

....

....

....

August

Examples: Homemade Vanilla Extract, page 96 ....

Honey-Lemon Jelly, page 94 ....

....

....

....

....

....

....

....

....

September

Examples: Bean-and-Pasta Soup Mix, page 77 ....

Fresh Mint Vinegar, page 87 ....

....

....

....

....

....

....

....

....

....

October

Examples: Easy Sweet-Tangy Mustard, page 92 ....

Spicy Jambalaya Mix, page 77 ....

....

....

....

....

....

....

....

....

....

November

Examples: Sour Cream Yeast Rolls, page 52 ....

Raspberry-Fudge Truffles, page 126 ....

....

....

....

....

....

....

....

....

December

Examples: Creamy Ham Casseroles, page 66 ....

Spicy Cocoa Snaps, page 169 ....

....

....

....

....

....

....

....

....

Measuring Up

Measure ingredients accurately so your recipes will turn out the way you want. Not all ingredients are measured with the same type of equipment. Just follow these guidelines:

Measure liquids in glass or clear plastic measuring cups with rims above the last cup level to prevent spilling. Place the cup on a level surface (don't pick the cup up), and fill with liquid.

Measure dry ingredients in metal or plastic measuring cups that hold the exact amount called for in the recipe. When measuring brown sugar, pack it firmly into the cup.

Measure flour by spooning it lightly into a dry measuring cup and letting it mound slightly; then level the top with a flat edge.

Cake flour is the only flour that needs sifting before measuring; others are pre-sifted.

A tiny ice cream scoop is a handy gadget that makes dropping dough onto cookie sheets a breeze (above). And you're guaranteed that all the cookies will be the same size.

High-Altitude Baking Adjustments

Cakes are affected by the lower air pressure at high altitudes more than any other type of baked good. When baked above 3,000 feet, cakes will not rise properly and may be dry and tough. Use this chart as a guide when baking cakes at high altitudes. In addition, when baking a cake above 3,000 feet in altitude, increase the baking temperature by 25 degrees.

Ingredients	3,000 ft.	5,000 ft.	7,000 ft.
Sugar: for each cup, decrease	Up to 1 tablespoon	Up to 2 tablespoons	Up to 3 tablespoons
Liquid: for each cup, add	1 to 2 tablespoons	2 to 4 tablespoons	3 to 4 tablespoons
Baking Powder: for each teaspoon, decrease	⅛ teaspoon	⅛ to ¼ teaspoon	¼ teaspoon

Smart Packaging

Great-tasting recipes become even more special
when attractively packaged for giving.

- **Package soft, chewy cookies** in containers that allow air to pass through, like cardboard bakery boxes. For a personal touch, collect Chinese take-out boxes, and decorate them with rubber stamps. (The stamps are available in many designs in variety stores.)

- Other creative containers for **soft, chewy cookies** include hat boxes, shoe boxes, Shaker boxes, or produce crates. Place waxed paper between each layer of cookies. If packaging cookies in crates, first wrap them in plastic wrap.

- **Package crisp cookies,** hard candies, and crunchy savory nibbles in airtight containers like metal tins. Crisp foods will absorb moisture from the air if not stored in airtight containers.

- Embellish **small metal coffee tins** for packaging tiny truffles or other candies. Replace plastic tops to seal.

- Consider using an **empty potato chip canister** for packaging. Cover it with Christmas wrapping paper. Fill with crisp cookies, candies, or salty snacks, and replace its plastic top to seal. These canisters provide a little protection for mailed gifts.

- **Fill a Christmas stocking** with a favorite snack mix or nut mix. Just package the mix in a large resealable plastic bag and tuck it and holiday napkins into the stocking.

- **Top off decorative jars of homemade dessert sauces** with raffia or decorative ribbon and bows. Attach a homemade gift tag and an antique spoon. You can find collections of small spoons at flea markets and tag sales.

- **Bake and transport homemade breads** in light-weight recyclable aluminum pans available at most supermarkets. Wrap pans of bread with a large linen napkin. Or place bread in gift bags, and tie with ribbon.

- When giving a variety of foods together, **personalize a gift basket.** Include items to be eaten with your goodies or utensils that might be needed for further preparation. For example, package stone ground crackers and a block of cream cheese to serve with relish or chutney; or place bagels and a slicer alongside a gift of homemade preserves. Include a decorative butter knife, cookie cutters, hot-pads, or a set of coasters. Round out your basket with flavored coffee or tea.

Recommended Storage

In Your Pantry

Packaged Mixes

Cake mix	1 year
Casserole mix	18 months
Frosting mix	8 months
Pancake mix	6 months

Staples

Baking powder and baking soda	1 year
Flour	
All-purpose	10 to 15 months
Whole wheat, refrigerated	3 months
Milk	
Evaporated and	
sweetened condensed	1 year
Peanut butter	6 months
Salt, pepper, sugar	18 months
Vegetable shortening	8 months
Spices (Discard if aroma fades.)	
Ground	6 months
Whole	1 year

In Your Refrigerator

Dairy

Butter and margarine	1 month
Buttermilk	1 to 2 weeks
Cheese	
Soft, fresh cheeses	1 week
Aged cheeses	2 to 6 weeks
Eggs	1 month
Half and half	7 to 10 days
Milk	1 week
Sour cream	3 to 4 weeks
Whipping cream	10 days

In Your Freezer

Quick Breads

Loaves, muffins, biscuits, coffee cakes, crêpes, pancakes, waffles	Up to 3 months

Yeast Breads

Loaves, rolls	Up to 3 months
Coffee cakes, sweet rolls	3 months
Doughnuts	1 month

Cakes

Unfrosted	Up to 6 months
Frosted with cooked frosting	not recommended
Frosted with creamy-type frosting	2 to 3 months
Cheesecakes	2 to 3 months

Cookies

Unfrosted cookies	8 to 12 months

Pastries

Cream puff shells	1 month
Puff pastry	2 to 3 months

Pies

Pastry shell	2 to 3 months
Fruit	1 to 2 months
Pumpkin	2 to 4 months
Custard, cream, meringue	not recommended

Dairy

Butter	6 months
Cheese	4 months
Ice cream	1 to 3 months
Eggs	
Whites	6 months
Yolks	8 months

Metric Equivalents

The recipes that appear in this cookbook use the standard United States method
for measuring liquid and dry or solid ingredients (teaspoons, tablespoons, and cups).
The information in the following charts is provided to help cooks outside the U.S.
successfully use these recipes. All equivalents are approximate.

Metric Equivalents for Different Types of Ingredients

A standard cup measure of a dry or solid ingredient will vary in weight depending on the type of ingredient. A standard cup of liquid is the same volume for any type of liquid. Use the following chart when converting standard cup measures to grams (weight) or milliliters (volume).

Standard Cup	Fine Powder (ex. flour)	Grain (ex. rice)	Granular (ex. sugar)	Liquid Solids (ex. butter)	Liquid (ex. milk)
1	140 g	150 g	190 g	200 g	240 ml
¾	105 g	113 g	143 g	150 g	180 ml
⅔	93 g	100 g	125 g	133 g	160 ml
½	70 g	75 g	95 g	100 g	120 ml
⅓	47 g	50 g	63 g	67 g	80 ml
¼	35 g	38 g	48 g	50 g	60 ml
⅛	18 g	19 g	24 g	25 g	30 ml

Useful Equivalents for Dry Ingredients by Weight

(To convert ounces to grams, multiply the number of ounces by 30.)

1 oz	=	1/16 lb	=	30 g
4 oz	=	¼ lb	=	120 g
8 oz	=	½ lb	=	240 g
12 oz	=	¾ lb	=	360 g
16 oz	=	1 lb	=	480 g

Useful Equivalents for Length

(To convert inches to centimeters, multiply the number of inches by 2.5.)

1 in			=	2.5 cm	
6 in	=	½ ft	=	15 cm	
12 in	=	1 ft	=	30 cm	
36 in	=	3 ft = 1 yd	=	90 cm	
40 in			=	100 cm	= 1 m

Useful Equivalents for Liquid Ingredients by Volume

¼ tsp					=	1 ml
½ tsp					=	2 ml
1 tsp					=	5 ml
3 tsp	=	1 tbls		= ½ fl oz	=	15 ml
		2 tbls	= ⅛ cup	= 1 fl oz	=	30 ml
		4 tbls	= ¼ cup	= 2 fl oz	=	60 ml
		5⅓ tbls	= ⅓ cup	= 3 fl oz	=	80 ml
		8 tbls	= ½ cup	= 4 fl oz	=	120 ml
		10⅔ tbls	= ⅔ cup	= 5 fl oz	=	160 ml
		12 tbls	= ¾ cup	= 6 fl oz	=	180 ml
		16 tbls	= 1 cup	= 8 fl oz	=	240 ml
		1 pt	= 2 cups	= 16 fl oz	=	480 ml
		1 qt	= 4 cups	= 32 fl oz	=	960 ml
				33 fl oz	=	1000 ml = 1 L

Useful Equivalents for Cooking/Oven Temperatures

	Fahrenheit	Celsius	Gas Mark
Freeze water	32° F	0° C	
Room temperature	68° F	20° C	
Boil water	212° F	100° C	
Bake	325° F	160° C	3
	350° F	180° C	4
	375° F	190° C	5
	400° F	200° C	6
	425° F	220° C	7
	450° F	230° C	8
Broil			Grill

Handy Substitutions

Needed Ingredient	Substitution
Baking Products:	
Baking powder, 1 teaspoon	• ½ teaspoon cream of tartar plus ¼ teaspoon baking soda
Chocolate	
chips, semisweet, 1 package (6 ounces)	• 2 ounces unsweetened chocolate, 2 tablespoons vegetable shortening plus ½ cup sugar
semisweet, 1 ounce	• 1 ounce unsweetened chocolate plus 1 tablespoon sugar
unsweetened, 1 ounce or square	• 3 tablespoons cocoa plus 1 tablespoon butter or margarine
Cornstarch, 1 tablespoon	• 2 tablespoons all-purpose flour or granular tapioca
Corn syrup, light, 1 cup	• 1 cup sugar plus ¼ cup water
Flour	
all-purpose, 1 cup	• 1 cup plus 2 tablespoons sifted cake flour
cake, 1 cup sifted	• 1 cup sifted all-purpose flour, minus 2 tablespoons
self-rising, 1 cup	• 1 cup all-purpose flour, 1 teaspoon baking powder plus ½ teaspoon salt
Honey, 1 cup	• 1¼ cups sugar plus ¼ cup water
Marshmallow cream, 1 jar (7 ounces)	• 1 package (16 ounces) marshmallows, melted, plus 3½ tablespoons light corn syrup
Confectioners sugar, 1 cup	• 1 cup sugar plus 1 tablespoon cornstarch (all processed in food processor)
Tapioca, granular, 1 tablespoon	• 1 tablespoon all-purpose flour or 1½ teaspoons cornstarch
Dairy Products:	
Eggs, 2 large	• 3 small eggs
Whole milk, 1 cup	• ½ cup evaporated milk plus ½ cup water
Sour cream, 1 cup	• 1 cup plain yogurt plus 3 tablespoons melted butter or 1 cup plain yogurt plus 1 tablespoon cornstarch
Whipping cream, 1 cup	• ¾ cup milk plus ⅓ cup melted butter (for baking only; will not whip)
Yogurt, 1 cup	• 1 cup buttermilk
Seasonings and Spices:	
Allspice, 1 teaspoon ground	• ½ teaspoon ground cinnamon plus ½ teaspoon ground cloves
Apple pie spice, 1 teaspoon	• ½ teaspoon ground cinnamon, ¼ teaspoon ground nutmeg plus ⅛ teaspoon ground cardamom
Brandy, 1 tablespoon	• ¼ teaspoon brandy extract plus 1 tablespoon water
Ginger, crystallized, 1 tablespoon	• ⅛ teaspoon ground ginger
Orange peel, 1 tablespoon	• 1½ teaspoons orange extract or 1 tablespoon grated orange zest
Pumpkin pie spice, 1 teaspoon	• ½ teaspoon ground cinnamon, ¼ teaspoon ground ginger, ⅛ teaspoon ground allspice plus ⅛ teaspoon ground nutmeg
Vanilla bean, 1 (1 inch)	• 1 teaspoon vanilla extract

Recipe Index